FOLLOWING CHRIST

A LENTEN READER TO STRETCH YOUR SOUL

CARMEN ACEVEDO BUTCHER

PARACLETE PRESS
Brewster, Massachusetts

Following Christ: A Lenten Reader to Stretch Your Soul

Copyright © 2010 by Carmen Acevedo Butcher

ISBN 978-1-55725-540-2

Library of Congress Cataloging-in-Publication Data

Following Christ : a lenten reader to stretch your soul / [selected and edited by] Carmen Acevedo Butcher.
       p. cm.
  Includes bibliographical references.
  ISBN 978-1-55725-540-2
  1. Lent. 2. Stations of the Cross. I. Butcher, Carmen Acevedo.
  BV85.F615 2010
  232.96--dc22   2009030990

10 9 8 7 6 5 4 3 2 1

Published by Paraclete Press
Brewster, Massachusetts
www.paracletepress.com
Printed in the United States of America

May these wise words shine
on our wintry souls,
frozen by loneliness and hurt,
and thaw us.

CONTENTS

Nothing is so beautiful as spring.
—GERARD MANLEY HOPKINS

After days of endless, sunless cold, another morning dawns and I balk, blue plastic scraper in hand, at the thought of scratching ice from my windshield one more time, pausing instead to scan still barren trees for tiny, tight green furls against the gray. Tired of heavy long johns, turtlenecks, wool sweaters, thick socks, gloves, hats, mufflers, big coats, and cramped dark days inside, our sluggish souls crave the pilgrimage toward light and hope. We wait for that first purple crocus, and count down the days until we can throw on a T-shirt, shorts, and sandals.

This kind of eager waiting is the essence of Lent, that forty-day period between Ash Wednesday and Easter Sunday. *Lent* was first spelled *lencten*, the Old English word for "springtime," rooted in the verb *lengan*, "to become longer," which refers to the lengthening days we all greet with great joy as signals of nature's resurrection in lemon-yellow jonquils, sunny wisps of forsythia, and pink-and-lavender Japanese magnolias.

This seasonal shift is a compelling metaphor for those who want to be more spiritually authentic. As my friend George Thomason says, "Lent is so powerful in its stillness; I always feel like a seed in the cradle of the dark winter earth, tense with expectation." Lent is the season for being still, for waiting in the dark on that first soft light of spring.

THE TRANSFORMATIVE DISCIPLINE OF WAITING ON GOD

To the ancient church, Lent's forty days symbolized obedience—waiting on God. The most well-known biblical models of this intentional patience are Moses, Elijah, and Jesus. Each fasted forty days in solitude, were tested and purified, and lived out this truth: "Therefore the LORD waits to be gracious to you; therefore he will rise up to show mercy to you. For the LORD is a God of justice; blessed are all those who wait for him."

We want wholeness, too, so we wait, stretching our souls toward the sun of God's forgiveness. Alone with God, we dare new surrenders that can heal us and make us whole. The imminent greening of God's creation feels like a personal invitation. It is the time of Lent. We listen.

In this Lenten reader, we hear from many rich voices of those who waited on God long before us. From well-known writers to lesser-known mystics and even an Anonymous or two—all have been chosen because they spent their lives listening to and developing a relationship with the profound eloquence of God's silence and its twin, loving others. The sixteenth-century Spanish mystic John of the Cross once said, "Silence is God's first language." Learning how to listen to God's silence is the crux of this devotional.

In these pages we find the life-changing wisdom of Francis of Assisi, Hildegard of Bingen, John Donne, Dante, Thomas à Kempis, Richard Rolle, Bernard of Clairvaux, and even Anglo-Saxon writers. We listen to the sagacity of saints like Benedict, Augustine, Gregory, Bonaventure, Anthony, and Ignatius. We learn from mystics like Julian of Norwich, Catherine of Siena, Teresa of Avila, Richard of St. Victor, Mechthild of Magdeburg, Gertrude the Great, Birgitta of Sweden, and Umiltà of Faenza. We drink in the enduring words of Desert Fathers and Mothers such as Abba (Father) Poemen, Amma (Mother) Theodora, and John Cassian. To introduce you further to each voice behind the quoted material, a short biography for each is provided in Appendix A.

Their voices cross the centuries. Their insights stretch from the oral traditions of the Egyptian deserts to the styli-scratched, brown-iron-gall-inked vellum manuscripts preserving sermons, poems, and rich devotional literature to the brilliant printed works of the Renaissance. Our ancient mentors never knew our jittery, vertigo-inducing wireless world, but, because each was a person of prayer, their words reveal why we have every reason to wait on God with great joy, in all circumstances. Their tried-and-true principles can guide us through our post-postmodern broadband jungle, showing us the enduring value of Isaiah's words: "Those who wait for the LORD shall renew their strength, they shall mount up with wings like eagles, they shall run and not be weary, they shall walk and not faint."

THE STATIONS OF THE CROSS

This devotional offers a unique approach to participating in Lent. Its readings have been selected to reflect the themes of the Cross, such as obedience, humility, grace, godly sorrow, and redemption; these themes, in turn, are organized around the stations of the cross, also called the "way of the cross" (*Via Crucis*) or the "way of sorrow" (*Via Dolorosa*). One of the earliest Christian devotional exercises, the stations of the cross commemorates the passion and resurrection of our Lord Jesus Christ, with each station representing an event that took place during the last week of Jesus' life. First observed in the Middle Ages by Christian pilgrims visiting the Holy Land and the sites of Jesus' passion, its use has been encouraged through the centuries by leaders of the church—especially Franciscan and Jesuit monks—because walking the stations of the cross strengthens a pilgrim's faith in the God of love.

Devotion to these stations grew when they were adapted to meet the needs of many ancient pilgrims who could not travel to Jerusalem to walk the literal way of the cross—starting at the Garden of Gethsemane, on to the high priest's courtyard, to Pilate's house, through Jerusalem, out to the hill known as Calvary or Golgotha on which Jesus was crucified, and finally ending at the tomb. For Christians who could not physically make the journey to Jerusalem, a picture or a sculpture depicting each stage of Jesus' journey to the cross was erected in or near a local church or other public venue. During Lent, then, people walked from station to station, as they do today, immersing themselves in Bible verses and meditating on the meaning of Jesus' life, death, and resurrection in the hopes of living different, better, kinder, and more peaceful lives.

Over the years, this Catholic practice has been embraced by Christians of all denominations for its powerful ability to reintroduce us to the reality of Christ's abiding presence in our lives. No longer thought of in the same context as the corrupt indulgences of the Middle Ages, the stations of the cross are known by many to be a genuine devotional path. Protestants find this ancient practice allows them to connect with the stages of Christ's journey on earth, not on a superficial or emotional level, but in a profoundly transformative way. Anyone whose spiritual goal is learning how to imitate Christ's love-filled walk through darkness into light finds everlasting hope in the stations of the cross.

This book helps readers make this spiritual pilgrimage of prayer during Lent, or at any other time, by reminding that life is largely about making the journey of maturity. As we read 1 Corinthians, we are challenged to stop speaking, thinking, and reasoning like petty children, and to grow up. Our adventure into wisdom, like any trip we take, has many stops along the way, and we may think of these developmental stages as "stations." It is worth considering what a station is. Rooted in the Latin word meaning "to stand," *station* calls up the image of a person "standing" at a bus stop, waiting for the next bus to arrive. Stations, whether they are for buses, taxis, or trains, are places where people stop and wait, en route to somewhere else. Similarly, in this life, we are always waiting on God, en route to heaven. This devotional helps us learn to be kind to others waiting beside us at the bus stop.

Over the centuries, there have been different stations of the cross. Until recently, this list represented the fourteen traditional stations:

1. Jesus is condemned to death.
2. Jesus is handed his cross.
3. Jesus falls for the first time.
4. Jesus meets his mother.
5. Simon of Cyrene is required to carry Jesus' cross.
6. Veronica wipes the face of Jesus.
7. Jesus falls a second time.
8. Jesus meets the women of Jerusalem.
9. Jesus falls a third time.
10. Jesus is stripped of his clothes.
11. Jesus is crucified.

12. Jesus dies on the cross.

13. Jesus' body is taken down from the cross.

14. The body of Jesus is placed in the tomb.

In the twentieth century, there was a profound shift in the makeup of the stations of the cross, away from legend and toward a solely scriptural foundation. In 1991, Pope John Paul II made this change official when he deleted from this traditional stations list those events not found in the Scriptures, replacing them with other stations taken directly from the Gospel accounts of Jesus' life. The resulting list of the stations of the cross by Pope John Paul II includes fourteen stations entirely based on the Bible in their commemoration of the passion of Jesus.

Megan McKenna outlines these modern scriptural stations in her book *The New Stations of the Cross: The Way of the Cross According to Scripture*:

1. Jesus prays in the Garden of Gethsemane.

2. Jesus is betrayed by Judas.

3. Jesus is condemned to death by the Sanhedrin.

4. Jesus is denied by Peter.

5. Jesus is judged by Pilate.

6. Jesus is scourged and crowned with thorns.

7. Jesus carries his cross.

8. Jesus is helped by Simon of Cyrene.

9. Jesus meets the women of Jerusalem.

10. Jesus is crucified.

11. Jesus promises to share his reign with the good thief.

12. Jesus is on the cross, with his mother and disciple below.

13. Jesus dies on the cross.

14. Jesus is placed in the tomb.

McKenna and many other devotional writers today add a fifteenth station, "Jesus rises from the dead." This Lenten book follows their lead because the gospel is literally the "Good News" of Christ—the *godspel* in Old English, from *god* ("good") and *spel* ("story, message"). Any devotional practice must take us through darkness bravely and into the light of love.

THOMAS MERTON ON THE DANGER OF LOVING

This book that you now hold is quite serious about leading you (and me) further along the path of love, which always seems to require a genuine encounter with and intimate study of the Bible. Therefore, interwoven with the sage words of ancient Christians here we also find Bible passages pointing us to Christ's life and wisdom. As discussed later in this introduction, we will not simply be reading these Bible verses; we will be "eating" them in the ancient practice known as the *lectio divina*, a slow "divine reading" of Scripture that feeds our souls.

The monk Thomas Merton reminds us of the power of such scriptural reflection: "Any serious reading of the Bible means personal involvement in it, not simple mental agreement with abstract propositions. And involvement is dangerous, because it lays one open to unforeseen conclusions."

Merton's use of "dangerous" here suggests—not the going-over-a-cliff-in-a-car kind of physical peril—but the very real invisible risks involved in any close personal relationship, such as the intimacy that we have with Christ. It is the danger a person feels who has not only fallen in love but who chooses to stand at an altar, promising to be faithful and true to his or her beloved—for better, for worse; for richer, for poorer; in sickness and in health—and to love and to cherish until death. In a commitment to love, things shift inside your soul. You start struggling with long-held prejudices. You give up and give over and see the world differently as your world weaves with another's.

This book is meant to take us on this dangerous journey. As we meditate on God's Word, walking the stations of the cross through the journey of prayer, we grow more intimate with the Lord of peace. Becoming better friends with God, we also notice that this spiritual pilgrimage keeps us close to the nourishing paradox of our faith—Christ's cross. As Matthew writes in his Gospel: "For those who want to save their life will lose it, and those who lose their life for my sake will find it. For what will it profit them if they gain the whole world but forfeit their life? Or what will they give in return for their life?" Christ's suffering is at the heart of all we do, and if we want to be in a relationship with Jesus, we must follow in his footsteps.

The wise men and women quoted in this book teach us how to be passionate about loving God, ourselves, and others, never forgetting that "passion" is rooted in the Latin *patior*, "to suffer." They show us we too can pick up a painful cross and follow Christ on the steps of his journey. Being faithful to Christ, even in the most painful circumstances, is possible. The witness of these men and women gives us the confidence

to try. Even as Thomas à Kempis acknowledges the
unending nature of our suffering, he encourages us
with his observations in *Imitation of Christ* about
how the risen, once-crucified Lord in us makes
the impossible possible:

> If you want to grow the faith of your soul, read
> Scripture with humility and simplicity, never
> making it your goal to gain a reputation for being
> "learned." Also read the wise words of ancient
> Christians attentively, and let them work their
> purpose in you. For the wiser a person is and
> the simpler the heart, the more Christ's light
> can enter into a person's life, and that which
> seems naturally impossible to us becomes
> possible through Christ's grace. So do not be
> discouraged when a problem arises. Consider
> painful circumstances helpful. They're good for
> your soul. Instead, let Christ strengthen you
> with his heavenly courage.

This Lenten devotional reminds us that our *passionate*
friend "suffers with" us daily. It is perhaps the sweetest-tast-
ing wisdom—Christ's constant, strengthening presence
in our lives. John of the Cross promises that quiet times
with God lead to real happiness even in struggle:

We use ladders for climbing, to reach things we need. In the same way, the soul climbs through the usefulness of contemplation and its mysteries up to divine knowledge, our greatest necessity. David sang about this in the Psalms: "Happy are those whose strength is in you, in whose heart are the highways to Zion. They go from strength to strength." The treasure at the top of the ladder is God. He is the only one who can make us happy.

Page after page, these ancient souls direct us back to Christ. As Karol Wojtyla wrote before he became Pope John Paul II, "I am a wayfarer on the narrow pavement of earth and I do not put aside the thought of Your face, which the world does not reveal to me."

LENT'S COMPASSIONATE ALERTNESS

Lent is also a time of penance, of repairing our relationship with God and with our neighbor. The Lenten themes for the stations of the cross reflect the penitent nature of this path:

• STATION 1 •
Jesus prays in the Garden of Gethsemane
THE WAKING OF PRAYER

• STATION 2 •
Jesus is betrayed by Judas
THE CHOICE OF OBEDIENCE

• STATION 3 •
Jesus is condemned to death by the Sanhedrin
THE PURIFYING OF SELF-EXAMINATION

• STATION 4 •
Jesus is denied by Peter
THE HEALING OF HUMILITY

• STATION 5 •
Jesus is judged by Pilate
THE GIFT OF GRACE

• STATION 6 •
Jesus is scourged and crowned with thorns
THE DARKNESS OF SUFFERING
AND ITS MEANING

• STATION 7 •
Jesus carries his cross
THE BEAUTY OF ENDURANCE

• STATION 8 •
Jesus is helped by Simon of Cyrene
THE NECESSITY OF FRIENDSHIP

• STATION 9 •
Jesus meets the women of Jerusalem
THE KNOWLEDGE OF GODLY SORROW

• STATION 10 •
Jesus is crucified
THE FORGIVING SACRIFICE

• STATION 11 •
Jesus promises to share his reign with the good thief
THE JOY OF REDEMPTION

• STATION 12 •
Jesus is on the cross, with his mother and disciple below
THE COMMUNITY OF AGAPE LOVE

• STATION 13 •
Jesus dies on the cross
THE TRUST OF LISTENING

• STATION 14 •
Jesus is placed in the tomb
THE BIRTH OF COURAGE

• STATION 15 •
Jesus rises from the dead
THE PREPARATION ON EARTH FOR ETERNAL LIFE

This book provides you a devotional for every morning and evening of Lent, plus the seven Lenten Sundays, even though Sundays are not traditionally counted in the forty days of the season. These short devotionals open windows on the unchanging nature of divine kindness. They begin and end each day with words reconnecting us with the most important truth—God loves us.

Each of the fifteen stations is introduced by a Bible passage presenting the historical moment of that station, followed by other verses that transition the reader to a paragraph or two introducing that station's theme. Here's how this looks: Station One and its theme, "The Waking of Prayer," are introduced by a reading from Mark 14, where Jesus prays in the Garden of Gethsemane; following this passage is a verse from Genesis often read in Ash Wednesday services, "You are dust, and to dust you shall return" (Gen. 3:19); and then we read from Romans, "It is now the moment for you to wake from sleep" (Rom. 13:11). These latter two verses strengthen Station One's theme, reminding us that we are lethargic, mortal "dust," who need daily to seek a "waking" through prayer.

MAKING TIME FOR GOD IN
LECTIO DIVINA

This book helps us to meet with God during Lent, or at any time we wish to explore Christ's journey through the stations of the cross. Just set aside forty days (or a week, a few days, a day) as a private spiritual retreat. To start, you only need a few minutes after breakfast and several minutes before bed for peaceful reflection in the ancient monastic tradition of *lectio divina* or "divine reading." Since ancient times, this spiritual discipline has been compared to the ruminating eating behavior of certain animals. *Ruminate,* from the Latin *ruminare,* means "to chew the cud, turn over in the mind."

Lectio divina requires only two tools: Scripture (or any of the wise passages in this devotional) and a completely unhurried time of personal reflection. Instead of rushing through the text, you retreat to your favorite place. Sit down. Do whatever you need to be comfortable. Then just sit there and focus on Scripture.

Let's use Philippians 4:4–7 as an example. It is one of my favorite passages. I have often chewed on it in *lectio divina*–style reflection:

> Rejoice in the Lord always; again I will say, Rejoice. Let your gentleness be known to everyone. The Lord is near. Do not worry about anything, but in everything by prayer and supplication with thanksgiving let your requests be made known to God. And the peace of God, which surpasses all understanding, will guard your hearts and your minds in Christ Jesus.

STEP ONE

Lectio (Reading and Listening)

The practice of *lectio divina* has four simple steps. First, "take a bite." Read the passage slowly, letting your attention settle where it wants. Read the verses aloud if that helps you focus. As you listen, you will find that certain words or phrases have something to say to you. Let your soul gravitate to these. They will begin speaking to you.

In these verses from Philippians, I am drawn to the word *Rejoice*. It is not presented as an option, but a requirement—I *must* "rejoice in the Lord" (v. 4a). As if I did not hear this command well enough, Paul says again, "Rejoice" (v. 4b).

But how? is the question my spirit raises. I keep reading, and my question is immediately answered in the text: "Let your gentleness be known to everyone" (v. 5). *Be gentle. Rejoicing and being gentle rarely come naturally to me, but Scripture suggests they are interconnected. Do one, you get the other. Mother always said, "Count your blessings." Could counting my blessings and thanking God make me gentler?*

I keep reading, slowly. The next verses in Philippians instruct me not to worry: "Do not worry about anything" (v. 6a). *Anything? How?* "In everything by prayer and supplication with thanksgiving let your requests be made known to God" (v. 6b). *I should turn to you. Ask you. Confide in you. Be thankful.* "And the peace of God, which surpasses all understanding, will guard your hearts and your minds in Christ Jesus" (v. 7). *Peace will "guard" my heart against the onslaught of worry if I thank God for my blessings and also confide in him with my troubles.*

STEP TWO

Meditatio (Meditation)

Scripture comes mysteriously and powerfully alive when we slow ourselves in it. The second step is *meditation*, when we stop to reflect on the passage. Continuing the metaphor of feeding on the Word, next we "chew" the Scripture passage. Obviously, I engage in some of this reflection during step one, but this is fine because the different stages of *lectio divina* are not rigid categories. They compose a fluid process of discovery.

In step two, however, this reflection intensifies. Try to enter the passage or verse you have read. Pay careful attention to the words. In this passage from Philippians, I find that the verbs, "rejoice," "do [not] worry," and "will guard," as well as the nouns, "gentleness," "prayer," "thanksgiving," "peace," and "Christ" are spiritually nourishing, but the word that most sticks to the ribs of my soul is a small one, the preposition "in," appearing three times: "Rejoice *in* the Lord always"; "Do not worry about anything, but *in* everything by prayer and supplication with thanksgiving let your requests be made known to God"; and "the peace of God, which surpasses all understanding, will guard your hearts and your minds *in* Christ Jesus." This preposition, "in," gives the verbs their Christocentric power: if I rejoice *in* the Lord always and *in* everything thank God, telling him about my anxieties and stress, I will be guarded by God's peace *in* Christ.

In *lectio divina*, also let your mind, your memories, your imagination, your emotions, and your life experiences engage with the verses. Sit silently and pay attention to the things that come to you. Ask God, "What can I learn from this verse?" Or, "How can it heal me?" Or, "How can I live out this truth?"

If the passage is a story, such as the prodigal son parable, ask yourself who you are in the story. Are you the father looking for a lost loved one, the rebellious and estranged child, or the sullen elder son? Or, in a different story, imagine that you are the leper miraculously healed by Jesus. What was this encounter with divine healing like? Let yourself ask questions such as: *Who is Jesus? What was my life like before I met Christ? How did being with him make me feel? How is my life different now that I know his healing? What must I do now?*

This period of reflection can also be emotional. The passage from Phillipians 4 reminds me how much of my life I have spent worrying and complaining, *not* rejoicing. That makes me sad. So I sit with that sadness awhile and let the verse become personal to me. This Bible verse is no longer an abstract truth telling everybody else to rejoice; as I listen to it, it is talking to me personally. It is saying to *me*, "Rejoice."

Then I find myself analyzing why I stop rejoicing so often in my daily life. Why am I often down? One reason is I work too hard and find resting difficult; therefore, I am exhausted much of my life. I am reminded—not for the first time in my type A–style life—that learning to rest is the key to my soul's health. I have never needed a scholarly commentary to know this truth; by slowing down and engaging in *lectio divina*, I realize over and over that learning to rest in Christ ought to become my life's work.

This truth brings us to another point about this ancient practice. Save the intense use of excellent Bible commentaries for another time. Never give up the regular study of the Bible in the company of the best scholars, but there is no need to consult them during *lectio divina*, which is meant to be a personal encounter with Scripture. Your heart is authority enough for you in this discipline. Scripture will reveal itself to you if you open your soul to its promptings and let honesty be your favorite form of exegesis.

STEP THREE
Oratio (Prayer)

Then pray. "Savor" the Word. Reading Scripture in this way often stirs up feelings, memories, hurts, inexpressible joy, and, yes, a multitude of worries. Give your emotions and your ghosts and your pain and your fear to God. Name them, one by one. Or let them lump themselves into a single yearning, and speak that. "God, help me" always works. Or, "Christ, I am sick; heal me." Or some passage that you read may fill you with joy. Then rejoice. Thank God. How often in the hours of a day do we say, "Thank you, God."

Or you may find your sorrow too profound for words or your gratitude too great for anything but silence. In either case, the Holy Spirit prays for us, as Paul says. When we falter, the Spirit helps us; when we do not know how to pray, God's Spirit intercedes for us "with sighs too deep for words."

It can also happen that you do not feel anything much at all. That response is also valid. It does not signal that your time of *lectio divina* has failed. No two times of *lectio divina* are alike. Simply trust in God's direction through this time and move on to step four.

STEP FOUR
Contemplatio (Contemplation)

The final step is surrender. "Digest" the Word. Here we do that hard work of letting go and resting in God. The Christian authors quoted in this book understood that we starve spiritually unless we embrace the quiet the psalmist recommends. With this book, we can make God's love our "hiding place" and listen to our Creator as he invites us into a deeper intimacy with him: "Be still, and know that I am God!"

This next step of not-thinking is difficult for many. I who am addicted to the overanalyzing synonymous with "worrying" find that my excuse for not surrendering in the quiet to God's still presence is that I am a harried middle-aged woman trying to meet book deadlines and also be present to raise a teenager and a third grader with gentle, firm love. What's your excuse?

If we sit in *lectio divina* for a few minutes each day (additionally, I love to walk in *lectio divina* with a Bible verse typed on a notecard), we soon find that our hungry, wireless-world souls are truly fed by this ancient practice first taught by Benedict of Nursia one and a half millennia ago.

IDENTIFYING WITH CHRIST

These devotionals organized around the stations of the cross are the blossoms of *lectio divina*, practiced by the spiritual authors presented here, who sat with, waited on, listened to, and longed for God. By spending time with them, we learn how to make these words from Matthew a reality for our lives: "If any want to become my followers, let them deny themselves and take up their cross and follow me." Sitting in silence with these close friends of Christ, we travel directly through our own soul's struggles—fear, betrayal, disappointment, condemnation, injustice, suffering, burdens, godly sorrow, sacrifice, redemption, humility, community, trust, grief, and the triumphant joy of love.

When through *lectio divina* we enter into the space where the God-man Jesus lives, we also begin identifying with the Christ who loves us intimately, which is to say, we begin to follow him spiritually. Station by station, here is our Christocentric journey through this book: Station One—in difficult times, we walk with Jesus into the waking prayer of the Garden of Gethsemane. Station Two—when we are betrayed, as Christ is by his disciple Judas, we understand that obedience is always a choice with profound consequences. Station Three—when we find ourselves judging others, as the most powerful religious leaders (the Sanhedrin) condemn Jesus, we seek the purifying self-examination that can teach us how to love others. Station Four—when we experience abandonment, as Christ does when his close friend Peter denies ever having known him, we remember that only through humility can our own self-centeredness be healed.

Station Five—when life seems unfair to us, we remember that the sinless, silent Christ understands, standing before the cowardly Pilate's injustice and slander, and we pray for the gift of God's grace to strengthen us in our decisions.

Station Six—when we walk through physical pain and humiliation, we contemplate that Christ is scourged and crowned with thorns, and his acceptance of suffering and presence in our pain give it meaning. Station Seven—when our problems seem weighty, we see Christ picking up his own heavy cross and are encouraged by the beauty of his endurance. Station Eight—when we are overwhelmed by life's hardships, we see Simon of Cyrene shouldering Christ's cross, and are reminded of the necessity of friendship, of shouldering someone else's burdensome cross and carrying it for them, and of letting a friend do the same for us. Station Nine—when we know the deep pangs of spiritual regret, instead of refusing this maturing knowledge, we embrace it, remembering that Jesus listens to the grieving women of Jerusalem and urges them to focus instead on learning godly sorrow. Station Ten—when our sinfulness deadens our souls, we look to the cross, where Christ's sacrifice makes our forgiveness possible.

Station Eleven—when we behave in a way that breaks God's law, we are beckoned to turn to Christ, as the good thief does, and find there the joy of our redemption. Station Twelve—in every situation, we should encourage community, imitating Christ's concern on the cross for his mother Mary and disciple John by living out agape love. Station Thirteen—when our souls are desolate and God seems dead, we desperately need to fix our eyes on Christ's victory on the cross, never losing our trust in God and remaining faithful by listening to him. Station Fourteen—and when our prayers seem dry and our hearts afraid, we remember that Christ is in the tomb for a reason, to give birth to our courageous hearts. Station Fifteen—finally, we rejoice at seeing Christ emerge alive and whole from the grave and know that he lives in us now, strengthening us as on earth we prepare our souls for eternal life.

WALKING THROUGH THE STATIONS

As we contemplatively read through the stations of the cross, we do well to remember why we make this meditative journey. As Father Laurence Freeman pointed out in a sermon for All Souls Day at the

Benedictine Priory in Montreal, "Every time we meditate, we participate in the death of Christ." This quiet "mini-death" gives our souls a taste of the wisdom of Paul's beautiful hymn in the book of Philippians, where he describes the *kenosis* ("emptying") that each of us must experience if we want to imitate Christ:

> If then there is any encouragement in Christ, any consolation from love, any sharing in the Spirit, any compassion and sympathy, make my joy complete: be of the same mind, having the same love, being in full accord and of one mind. Do nothing from selfish ambition or conceit, but in humility regard others as better than yourselves. Let each of you look not to your own interests, but to the interests of others. Let the same mind be in you that was in Christ Jesus, who, though he was in the form of God, did not regard equality with God as something to be exploited, but emptied himself, taking the form of a slave, being born in human likeness. And being found in human form, he humbled himself and became obedient to the point of death—even death on a cross.

PRAYING WITH A NAKED INTENT

In a slender fourteenth-century masterpiece on prayer, *The Cloud of Unknowing*, an anonymous English monk explains how we can make ourselves humbly available to God in prayer. Taking his advice, we can let it guide us along the way of the cross here and now. Anonymous says, "Be bold" reading, walking, and praying through these stations of the cross. He also tells us we only need *a nakid entente* ("a naked intent") if we want an authentic walk with God. In other words, if we desire with all our heart to be close to God, that is enough. Simply reach out to the never-aloof God, and discover the truth of St. Augustine's words: "God is closer to your soul than you are yourself."

This is how the stations of the cross become second nature to us—when we begin to realize that Christ's crucifixion and resurrection were both events in history and an ongoing, mysterious truth that can be lived out in our own lives. When we see that we can go beyond our own needs and desires and start serving others and even praying for and doing good to our enemies (without becoming doormats), then the stations of the cross have seeped into the very marrow of our souls, becoming revealed truth about the nature of our long-suffering, always faithful, all-powerful God. The stations can become our constant companions, reminders that God is intent on loving us, even though we reject him and his deep love.

The entries of this Lenten devotional book are arranged to imitate the rhythm of redemption; therefore, some of the stations have more readings than others, to emphasize certain themes. Throughout the book, the thematic motion is from darkness to light, from sin to forgiveness, from brokenness to healing, from godly sorrow to joy—with a circular rhythm that we recognize in the coming and going of the seasons. As the sun is the constant in nature, so this book's recurring call to prayer guides our souls through winter into certain springtime.

May we discover in the silence of this book what a friend we have in Jesus. May we find rest in Christ, whose experience on the dark hill of Golgotha reminds us that we have much work to do on earth, before the light of Easter may come at last. May we stop here and nurture our souls, learn to face our crosses fearlessly, trust Jesus for the strength we need, become bridge builders, and live out his healing.

As a last reminder of the transformative *lectio divina* approach recommended for this book, before reading each of the wise devotions in it, try praying these timeless words: "We adore you, Christ our Lord, and we praise you, because through your holy cross you redeemed the world."

Because these ancient works are meant for intelligent, spiritually hungry readers, they have been translated *sensum ex sensu* ("according to the sense"), not *verbum ex verbo* ("word for word"). This slow process means that I juggled choices of diction and syntax prayerfully while respecting the original message, to erase literalness and nurture ease of reading. This sort of translating is a kind of *scriptio divina*, a focused way of writing that can grow a writer's soul. The experience changed my life in a good way, and I am thankful for the witness of these vibrant Christians, especially for their wise words on reconciliation. I am also thankful to Christian Classics Ethereal Library (CCEL), online at http://www.ccel.org/, for its unparalleled resources in the Christian classics. CCEL's founder, Harry Plantinga, writes that the site's mission is to "build up the church by making classic Christian writings available and promoting their use." A word about the composite nature of some of the devotionals: sometimes this book combines different passages from one work so the thrust of that classic Christian text is presented; in these cases, ellipses have not been used. Also, unnumbered notes at the back of the book provide more material for those who want to dig deeper into the devotionals, exploring them further, and the quoted lead-ins help readers locate their position in the text.

Jesus prays
in the Garden of Gethsemane

THE WAKING OF PRAYER

They went to a place called Gethsemane [also called the Garden of Olives]; and he said to his disciples, "Sit here while I pray." He took with him Peter and James and John, and began to be distressed and agitated. And he said to them, "I am deeply grieved, even to death; remain here, and keep awake." And going a little farther, he threw himself on the ground and prayed that, if it were possible, the hour might pass from him. He said, "Abba, Father, for you all things are possible; remove this cup from me; yet, not what I want, but what you want." He came and found them sleeping; and he said to Peter, "Simon, are you asleep? Could you not keep awake one hour? Keep awake and pray that you may not come into the time of trial; the spirit indeed is willing, but the flesh is weak."
—Mark 14:32–38

[The LORD God said,] "You are dust, and to
dust you shall return."
—Genesis 3:19

Besides this, you know what time it is, how it is
now the moment for you to wake from sleep.
For salvation is nearer to us now than when
we became believers; the night is far gone,
the day is near. Let us then lay aside the works
of darkness and put on the armor of light.
—Romans 13:11–12

At the first station, we find Jesus despairing.
Mark tells us in his Gospel that Jesus is so upset that
he throws himself on the ground and prays. Taking
his spiritual agony to a quiet place, the Garden of
Gethsemane at the foot of the Mount of Olives, Jesus
shows us what to do when we despair—turn to God
in prayer. *Despair* means "hopeless," literally "without"
(*de-*) "hope" (*sperare*). The physician Gospel writer Luke
says Christ's agony is so great that he sweats great
drops of blood on the ground. This rare medical con-
dition, hematohidrosis, is caused by terrible stress.

Why is Christ beside himself with anguish? The
Son of God knows this is the night of his betrayal

and arrest. He faces crucifixion, the most painful and agonizingly slow form of physical and mental torture. He knows how weak we humans are, made of dust, for even his closest disciples are asleep; and he knows that the greatest agony of all will be accepting the suffering of humanity's sins—our heavy guilt—and that its weight will separate him from God.

See Jesus on the ground in the Garden of Olives understanding what his love is costing him. He shows us we must embrace the everyday battle that is prayer, and keep praying and never stop. The image is unforgettable: God is not distant. Christ has dirt on his knees. He knows anxiety. So we can follow him, he is praying in the garden. We must awake through prayer.

ASH WEDNESDAY MORNING

Always call on God in prayer. When dark thoughts come into our hearts, making us feel hopeless and depressed, they are sent by the devil, who is a conniving liar. He schemes against humanity and against God, hoping these negative thoughts will steal our faith in the mercy of God. We must never forget that despair cannot injure us if we do not give in to its perverse pleasure. We must reject these negative ideas by calling out to our Lord. If you have sinned, do not lose hope because of your error. Pray instead. On the other hand, if you have done something good, never presume too much on account of your goodness. Never congratulate yourself excessively. Never look down on someone else for sinning, and remember that when the wayward soul prays and repents of doing wrong, the Lord will raise that person up, as he did Lazarus.

—Ælfric of Eynsham: *Sermons*

ASH WEDNESDAY EVENING

Many people never wake from the sleep of this world. Lust lays heavy on their eyes and in their flesh, and they abuse the gospel with their immorality. We should instead be asking, "How can I live out my faith? How does repentance transform us? What does sincere godliness require? How can we learn Christlike living?"

Imitate Christ. Shake off the sleep of sin.

Rushing after the "best" education possible, we over-look the greatest teacher, Jesus. His humility and holy living are our best text. We should sit at his feet because his life can teach us everything. Everyone wants to "serve Christ," but it is hard to find anyone who chooses to follow him. Following is costly. We must be godly, modest, prone to listening, patient with others' faults, willing to suffer, and able to love difficult people.

This is hard. Sometimes we fall asleep spiritually. We are weak, but we can work hard. We can try imitating Christ in whatever we do. We can meditate on his godly life and work to be like him in loving others. We can try walking the path he walked. We need a certain brokenness of heart, as we know: "The poor have good news brought to them."

The only thing that opens our eyes is real regret. True regret starts deep within, and then spreads out, and finally we are able to see. If we want to become new creatures in Christ, we must steep ourselves in God's Word. It must mature in us like seeds that grow, producing spiritual fruits. God's Word can restore our souls, making our Adam natures shrivel and die; and Christ will live in us. We must do more than merely know God's Word. We must live it.

The world is exploding with information, but is anyone determined to know the love of the poor and humble Christ?

—Johann Arndt: *True Christianity*

A young man visited Abba Moses for a wise word, but the Abba gave him a question instead: "Why are you here? Go home. Sit in your cell. Prayer will teach you everything."

—*Sayings of the Fathers and Mothers*

THURSDAY MORNING AFTER ASH WEDNESDAY

The soul stays awake by seeing in three distinct, often overlapping ways. The first way is thinking. When the mind is thinking, though, it is easily distracted and usually less focused than during the second way, which is meditation, or when the mind is looking, caught between wonder and wisdom, waking up. The third way the soul stays awake is contemplation, when the soul is completely still, gazing on Truth.

When you are thinking, as you know, your mind is more likely to dash after every new idea popping into your head, although sometimes a long period of thinking can morph into meditation, or even into contemplation. Meditation and contemplation are superior to thinking because they desire wisdom. Contemplative prayer has the best vision of the three, penetrating this world's illusions to the reality of things, offering us epiphanies, giving us a taste of heaven. This is true prayer.

Those who quiet their souls in meditation and contemplation live with their eyes open, soaring through the day like birds. Their practice of stillness gives them wings, and they dart from here to there, sometimes hovering in midair on the unending motion of prayerful diligence. It is as if they are saying as they cling to the moment, "It is good for us to be here."

—Richard of St. Victor:

The Mystical Ark and *The Four Degrees of Violent Charity*
(or *The Four Degrees of Overwhelming Love*)

THURSDAY EVENING AFTER ASH WEDNESDAY

We ask the very first Beginning to open our eyes through the ineffable peace of Christ. But how can our souls dialogue with God? St. Francis prayed long hours in solitary places. One day as he prayed he saw an angel and Christ, and an awesome love melted his heart. He watched the seraph fly down from heaven on its six fiery wings, and suddenly he saw the man of God, crucified, there in the middle of its shining wings. This vision awed St. Francis, making him feel sad, thankful, and amazed, and it teaches us today that the mirror of contemplative prayer can reveal God to us. So, to live a godly life, always pray. When reading, ask God for inspiration. When questioning, ask God to help you stay loyal to him. When exploring the earth's wonders, ask God to help you cherish his mystery. When you work, ask for grace. When you study, ask God to teach you how to love. When you gain understanding, pray, "God, keep me humble." If we fall on our knees, we can give God our helplessness and failures.

Offer the One who loves you your shame.

—Bonaventure: *The Soul's Journey into God*

Whoever you are, regardless of your circumstances, you can turn from the stupor of self-will and join the Lord of all if you put on the strong armor of submission and serve Christ. Pray first before doing anything. The book of Romans tells us to wake up: "It is now the moment for you to wake from sleep." Open your eyes to the clear light revealing God's path to us. Open your ears to the intimate voice of God within, calling us to love. For the Gospel of John says, "Walk while you have the light, so that the darkness may not overtake you."

—Benedict: *Rule*

On the darkest night, I risked everything for love.
No one saw me, and I saw no one, quiet reigning,
I escaped down a hidden ladder at night.
I left my house when all was still,
my way lit only by my yearning.

The night was sweet, and nothing could
    show my way
through the darkness, except the inner light
    of prayer
shining brighter than the noonday sun,

guiding me until I found myself
in the loneliest place,
where the One I love
waited for me.

I know him well.

— John of the Cross: *Ascent of Mount Carmel*

Jesus is betrayed by Judas

THE CHOICE OF OBEDIENCE

Immediately, while he [Jesus] was still speaking, Judas, one of the twelve, arrived; and with him there was a crowd with swords and clubs, from the chief priests, the scribes, and the elders. Now the betrayer had given them a sign, saying, "The one I will kiss is the man; arrest him and lead him away under guard." So when he came, he went up to him at once and said, "Rabbi!" and kissed him. Then they laid hands on him and arrested him.
—Mark 14:43–46

[Jesus said,] "But among you there are some who do not believe." For Jesus knew from the first who were the ones that did not believe, and who was the one that would betray him. And he said, "For this reason I have told you that no one can come to me unless it is granted by the Father." Because of this many of his disciples turned back and no longer went about with him. So Jesus asked the twelve, "Do you also wish to go away?" Simon Peter answered

him, "Lord, to whom can we go? You have the
words of eternal life. We have come to believe
and know that you are the Holy One of God."
—John 6:64–69

At the second station, we find Jesus betrayed by
Judas. Mark tells us in his Gospel that Judas sends
Jesus to his death with a kiss. A kiss is the gesture
of intimacy. Can there be a crueler injury than
the disloyalty of one you love? Jesus knows the
humiliation of a failed relationship. He knows the
surprise of being abandoned by someone trusted,
for even when we know these things can happen,
who is ever prepared for them?

Judas commits the ultimate sin; he is unfaithful to
Christ's love. He lies to Jesus, the core of every sin.
In Dante's *Inferno*, the ninth circle of hell is reserved
for traitors who have had a special relationship with
the person they later abandoned. Of hell's concentric
circles, the ninth one is the lowest and innermost,
and the worst offenders are kept frozen and distorted
forever in its lake of ice known as the Cocytus, for
"wailing." Dante puts Judas here, near Cain. Only
Satan is farther in and lower down, at the very center
of hell.

Surely, and sadly, we see ourselves in Judas. We break our promises to Jesus and to those we love. Thank God for the forgiveness offered by Christ.

FRIDAY MORNING AFTER ASH WEDNESDAY

Jesus said, "But among you there are some who do not believe." The Gospel writer John reminds us in this verse that our allegiance to Christ is a personal choice.

"Because of [their unbelief] many of his disciples turned back and no longer went about with him." John does not say that some of Christ's followers "left" Jesus but that they "turned back." He is emphasizing that they physically cut themselves off from having a relationship with Jesus, severing their ability to strengthen their souls. When they stopped associating with Jesus, they abandoned their faith.

Then Jesus asked his inner circle, the twelve disciples, "Do you also wish to go away?" Jesus did not compliment them in an effort to convince them to stay with him. Nor did he beg his disciples to stay. Instead, Jesus showed true excellence as a teacher in this moment, because he wanted their motives to be pure. He wanted them to be drawn to his ministry, not to compliments. Christ never tries to manipulate emotions. He never tries to make us feel guilty. Nor did Jesus try to push his disciples away before any one of them could reject him. This would have separated them from him.

Instead, Jesus asked the Twelve, "Do you also wish to go away?" The wording of this question is extremely important because it removes all compulsion from the listener's mind. It allows the one being asked to make a personal choice. It is a question put by someone who does not want people attached to him through any sense of shame. Jesus wants the Twelve to stay with him only for love of him. Jesus shows wisdom here. With one gentle question, he gave the disciples the opportunity to make the right choice.

Jesus chose an unusual path in this situation. Neither complimenting his disciples, nor rejecting them, he asked them a question. Jesus asks us that same question today: "Do you also wish to go away?" This question is an act of love. It does not force. It is not coercion, a compelling someone to do something. In coercion there is no real connection, while love volunteers gladly.

Peter answered Jesus: "Lord, to whom can we go? You have the words of eternal life. We have come to

believe and know that you are the Holy One of God."
See how much Peter loved his Lord, so much so that
he did not think only of himself as he spoke. He did
not say "*I* know." He had his friends in mind when he
said, "*We* know that you are the Holy One of God."

Christ is community.

—John Chrysostom: *Sermon*

FRIDAY EVENING AFTER ASH WEDNESDAY

Our Lord gave us laws to guide us, but we create
"new" ones for ourselves, totally unlike God's. Our
self-conceived directives are at cross purposes with
divine teaching. We are opposing the wisdom of the
ages, but we are so stubborn that our self-will rebels
against everything good. Trampling God's commandments with arrogant behavior, we make our
lives difficult. There is nothing worse than betraying
Jesus, because this betrayal estranges us from God
and destroys community.

Love God. Abandon what is wrong.

—Ælfric of Eynsham: *Sermons*

Jesus says,

Learn obedience, or you will always be running from grace. Develop a contempt for your flaws if you wish to win the spiritual war for your soul. If you are mostly concerned with what you will receive in life, you lose the benefits of community. If you cannot, for sheer stubbornness, submit to your superior, your will is rebelling against me, because when you respect the wishes of a good manager, you learn to conquer your ego. This obedience integrates your soul and helps you deal with exterior temptations; otherwise, your inner self will always be disorganized. Discipline your soul because there is no worse enemy than your own self. Have you never noticed? Work to be in harmony with God's Spirit. Abdicate your throne. Remember that you are mortal and that I am omnipotent, but became the lowliest of the low so you can vanquish your lofty pride through my humility. Learn obedience.

—Thomas à Kempis: *Imitation of Christ*

SATURDAY MORNING AFTER ASH WEDNESDAY

Anybody who says, "I don't need a teacher," is arrogant. People who do not respect those who teach them in love, suffer from the worst disease of all—ignorance (the mother of arrogance). They will be taught, but unfortunately by the angels who fell from heaven, who ran from their good teachers there. Surely that path leads to misery.

God alone is the only one who needs no teacher. He has no beginning, and no one is above him. The rest of us, however, must learn. We need teachers. We are the creatures, not the Creator.

Teaching involves much more than words. Sometimes the most horrible person can be quite eloquent. Teaching is mostly about character. A cheerful outlook, an uncomplaining temperament, and a deciding to be thankful and bold—these traits teach and inspire others. If this were not so, the best teacher would never have told his disciples, as recorded in Matthew's Gospel, "Take my yoke upon you, and learn from me; for I am gentle and humble in heart." Christ did not say, "Learn to speak as I do" or "I will train you in rhetoric," but "Learn from me, for I am gentle and humble."

Obeying Christ is neither hard nor stressful. It only upsets those who hate being taught. To be a good student of God, we must either study what we do not know, or teach the things we do understand. If you do not feel like practicing either of these disciplines, you are being foolish. To tire of learning is a sign that you are losing faith. If you love God, you will be hungry to learn more about him. Walk in the spirit of power, love, and self-discipline.

Be brave. Mature by exploring the best knowledge of all and the best subject of all—Christ. May God help you in your quest for obedience.

—Palladius: *The Lausiac History*
(from the *Letter to Lausus the Chamberlain*)

SATURDAY EVENING AFTER ASH WEDNESDAY

A divine voice spoke to me, saying,

How fragile you are, Human, made of dust and grime, but I am the living Light. I make the darkness day, and I have chosen you to see great wonders, though I have humbled you on earth. You are often depressed and timid, and insecure. Because you are conscientious, you feel guilty, and chronic physical pain has thoroughly scarred you. But the deep mysteries of God have saturated you, too, and so has humility.

When I heard this Voice, I began trying to live a godly life. The path became difficult as I questioned myself again, saying, *This is pointless.* I wanted to soar. I dreamed impossible dreams and started projects I could never finish. I became dejected, so I sat and did nothing. My self-doubt is my greatest disobedience. It makes me miserable, and I struggle with this cross daily.

But God is by my side, reminding me that he created me. So, even in the middle of my depression, I walk with wise patience over the marrow and blood of my body. I am the lion defending itself from a snake, roaring and knocking it back into its hole. I will never let myself give in to the devil's arrows.

—Hildegard of Bingen: *Scivias*

FIRST SUNDAY MORNING OF LENT

Can there be any evil greater than what we find at home? Can we hope to find peace anywhere, if we have none within us? No one, not even the closest friend or family member, is as intimate as the powers of our soul, which seem to wage war on us as if they knew the harm our vices are inflicting on them.

That is why Jesus often said to his disciples, "Peace, peace." Believe me, if we have no peace ourselves and never work for peace at home, we will not find it in anyone else's house. By the blood which our Lord shed for us, stop this war, I beg you. Begin the work of maturity. That is true obedience. If you have already started walking the right path, do not let the battle turn you back. Remember a relapse is worse than a fall. It could ruin you.

Instead, trust in God's mercy, not in yourselves. Then you will see how his majesty leads you into the greatest happiness possible.

—Teresa of Avila: *Interior Castle*

FIRST SUNDAY EVENING OF LENT

St. Francis saw obedience as the process of learning to integrate wisdom with simplicity. Remember? Jesus said, "See, I am sending you out like sheep into the midst of wolves, so be wise as serpents and innocent as doves." But is it possible for anyone to truly be "obedient"? St. Francis answered this question:

Yes. Think of a corpse. You can put it anywhere you want. It will not say, "Stop that!" It does not argue when you move it from one place to another. It does not care where it is. If you put it on a throne or honor it in any way, it does not look down on others, for its eyes are dead to this world. And if you dress the corpse in royalty's deepest purple, its white skin merely looks whiter. Those obedient to Christ have this sort of humility: promotions, honors, and flattery only increase their modesty.

—Bonaventure: *The Life of St. Francis*

Jesus is condemned to death by the Sanhedrin

THE PURIFYING OF SELF-EXAMINATION

When day came, the assembly of the elders of the people, both chief priests and scribes, gathered together, and they brought him to their council. They said, "If you are the Messiah, tell us." He replied, "If I tell you, you will not believe; and if I question you, you will not answer. But from now on the Son of Man will be seated at the right hand of the power of God." All of them asked, "Are you, then, the Son of God?" He said to them, "You say that I am." Then they said, "What further testimony do we need? We have heard it ourselves from his own lips!"
—Luke 22:66–71

If we say that we have no sin, we deceive ourselves, and the truth is not in us. If we confess our sins, he who is faithful and just will forgive us our sins and cleanse us from all unrighteousness.
—1 John 1:8–9

At the third station, we find Jesus betrayed again, this time by the religious leaders of his day. Standing before the Sanhedrin, the supreme court of justice presided over by high priest Joseph Caiaphas, Christ is charged with blaspheming. In reality, the Sanhedrin is jealous of Jesus. They are envious of how he draws crowds, listening to his talk of God's love. Lepers, the lame, the insane, and the blind are attracted to him because he heals them. The irony is that the people with the highest religious standards here are petty; they hate the Son of God for being the center of attention, which is what they most crave. They hate Jesus for preaching the deep mercy of God's love.

This station reminds us that envy is the seed of hatred and murder. *Envy* means "to look sideways at" another, from the verb *videre* ("to look") and the prefix *in-* ("askance at"). It is what we do in our souls when we resent someone else's accomplishments or happiness. Narrowing our eyes, we twist our heads to the right, and scowl. Eventually, envy rots our souls and stresses our bodies.

If we can learn the difference between self-absorption and self-examination, we can learn to practice the good health of introspection. Then when we recognize the signs of envy as they arise in us, we can train ourselves to give these base feelings to God, rejoicing instead for those who succeed. We must also pray that we do not judge those who attack us out of jealousy. We must pray for them by name, asking God to bless them.

Station Three also reminds us that innocent people are at this present moment being condemned to horrific, often silent suffering. They are Jesus before the Sanhedrin, unjustly accused. We must ask, "What if the Sanhedrin had invested itself more in prayer?"

MONDAY MORNING, FIRST WEEK OF LENT

Souls without prayer resemble people whose bodies are paralyzed. They have hands and feet, but they cannot use them. Some souls have made themselves ill by focusing on nothing but earthly matters, until there seems no cure for them. They seem unable to find refuge in their own hearts. They have started acting like beasts. Who can help them? It seems hopeless, even though their souls have been given the richest gift of all, communion with God himself. Unless they try to understand and change their miserable situation,

their minds will become as unmoving as stone, just as
Lot's wife was turned into a pillar of salt for looking
back, disobeying God's command.

This paralysis occurs because some people do not
understand their own nature. Our self-knowledge
becomes warped if we let ourselves become self-
absorbed. We must work at prayerful self-reflection,
or it will come as no surprise when spiritual disasters
overwhelm us. The devil's snares are subtle and real, and
he uses them to keep us unaware of our weaknesses.

—Teresa of Avila: *Interior Castle*

MONDAY EVENING, FIRST WEEK OF LENT

Often we have no idea that we have made a mistake
or that we have hurt someone; however, where we are
blind, God sees everything we do and think. So we
must turn to God and let him judge us.

Look inside yourself. Search your soul for weakness,
identify your shortcomings, and create an internal
dialogue in which you imagine your loved ones
sitting there as you discuss your flaws with them and
analyze how you can improve your relationships.

Everyone needs an honest and merciful internal critic. Pretend that those who love you can see everything terrible that you do or think. This exercise should keep you from lying or from making bad decisions and living in shame. Keep a record of your thoughts as if you were required to give a report of them to your best friend on earth. This practice should help you make the dirty ones vanish. Self-examination also helps you embrace compassion and bear the burdens of others.

If we examine our souls regularly, we can learn to be kind to each other.

—Athanasius of Alexandria: *The Life of St. Anthony*

TUESDAY MORNING, FIRST WEEK OF LENT

Let me ask you something. Who can judge another person's actions? Very few have this authority. Passing judgment on another is a profound responsibility that must never be accepted lightly, and then only by those who care for others' souls. Whether their authority is ordained by the Church or is privately sanctioned by the Holy Spirit, those in the position of judging others must accept this burden in a loving, mature way.

We must never forget that judging a fellow human being is a terrible burden. Never assume that you have been chosen to take on this power. Never rush to judge anyone, and do not be a faultfinder. Speak to someone only if you feel the nudge of the Holy Spirit during long periods of prayer. Those who in their arrogance take on this responsibility will quickly find how easy it is for things to go wrong.

Beware. Judge yourself as you want. That is between you and God or your spiritual director.

But leave others alone.

—Anonymous: *Cloud of Unknowing*

TUESDAY EVENING, FIRST WEEK OF LENT

Sweet Jesus, hear my prayer. My soul is sick, as you know. I look inside and see that I suffer from temptation and anxiety. Help me. Stay with me as I sweat out this spiritual fever. For I am afraid. Send an angel to lay a cool hand on me.

Hear my prayer.

Why was it you, Lord, who was killed? It should have been me instead. Thank you for allowing yourself to be

tortured for my sake. Thank you for permitting yourself
to be bullied. Thank you for accepting betrayal and
humiliation. Thank you for taking the blows and the
nails. Thank you for enduring brutality and murder, for
me. Thank you for every step you took in sorrow.

I love you.

Thank you for letting blood drip down your face.

I love you.

Thank you for letting thorns slash your head.

I love you.

Thank you for accepting the spit
   from mouths cursing you.

Have mercy on us all. We love you.

—Richard Rolle: *Meditations*

WEDNESDAY MORNING, FIRST WEEK OF LENT

One day after church, Abba Macarius turned to the
brothers and shouted at them: "Run! Abandon this
world!"

Puzzled, one monk turned back, asking, "How?
Where can we go? We already live in the desert."

Abba Macarius pressed his finger to his lips, saying, "Do this," then went into his prayer room and slammed the door.

—*Sayings of the Fathers and Mothers*

Stop whatever you are doing. Go to a room where you can be all by yourself, and close the door. Enter the inner sanctum of your soul. Do not worry there. Do not think about all the things you have to do. Speak to your Creator, saying, "Your face, LORD, do I seek." In that private space, turn to Jesus. Say, "Jesus, like a mother, you gather us to you. With a mother's gentleness, you weep for our sins, cry for our arrogance, lead us out of hatred, deliver us from judging, comfort our sorrow, heal our wounds, and feed us pure milk. You are our mother, Lord. You gather us under your wings. You died for us and give us life. Restore our souls. Remake us in your peace."

—Anselm: *On the Existence of God,*
Song of Anselm, and *Prayer to St. Paul*

WEDNESDAY EVENING, FIRST WEEK OF LENT

Bring your heart before God. Offer it humbly to him, in love. If you wish to know God, contemplate nothing but his kindness. Turn inward. Forget everyone for the moment. Focus solely on God, and you will make him happy. Angels help you.

When you focus on God's compassion, your prayers benefit everyone in this world. Only people who spend time in quiet contemplation learn to love, and, conversely, only those who go out into the loud world and love others find contemplative time fruitful.

Leave stress outside the door of this spiritual exercise. Bring gentleness to it. Bring humility. Wait on the Lord. Be patient. Be the tree, and let God's grace be the carpenter. Be the house, and let God's grace be the homeowner living there. Trust your deepest mind.

Remember your good manners before God. Avoid trying hard, do not be stubborn, and never be rude. As you begin, restrain your loud, impatient spirit. It is a beast, and if it seeks to touch this spiritual treasure, it will be beaten away with stones for its presumption.

Refuse to be the greedy greyhound. Never let hunger get the best of you. Learn self-control. Learn to love skillfully and without straining. Act as if you are in no hurry. Hide your eagerness from God, as if you do not want him to know how badly you want to see him. Perhaps I sound like I am teasing, but if you try this approach, you will experience God's playfulness, which is just like a father's joy when he is embracing and kissing his child.

If you want to focus your contemplative intent into one word, to make it easier, pick a word of one syllable, like *God* or *Love*. Select whatever little word helps you most. Do not choose a two-syllable word, rather keep it short, so it will focus your spirit on God. Fasten this syllable to your heart. In times of inner war, this little word will be your shield and spear.

When you enter contemplation, you will encounter the dark feeling of uncertainty that is the cloud of unknowing. This is a cloud you will experience no matter how much time you spend in the quiet, and no matter how experienced you become. Let yourself feel comfortable there. Rest and listen in this darkness. It will always stand between you and God. God eludes our seeking minds every time we try to grasp him, so we must learn to make our home in this darkness.

Without God's input, this contemplation would be impossible, but with the help of his grace, it is easy. There is no need to hesitate. Try the work of prayer. Your affection for God will grow as you meditate solely on him. When your naked free will reaches out to God in the most vulnerable openness, bent on knowing him, mystery happens.

—Anonymous: *Cloud of Unknowing*

Jesus is denied by Peter

THE HEALING OF HUMILITY

Now Peter was sitting outside in the courtyard.
A servant-girl came to him and said, "You also
were with Jesus the Galilean." But he denied it
before all of them, saying, "I do not now what
you are talking about." When he went out to
the porch, another servant-girl saw him, and
she said to the bystanders, "This man was
with Jesus of Nazareth." Again he denied it
with an oath, "I do not know the man." After a
little while the bystanders came up and said to
Peter, "Certainly you are also one of them, for
your accent betrays you." Then he began to
curse, and he swore an oath, "I do not know
the man!" At that moment the cock crowed.
Then Peter remembered what Jesus had said:
"Before the cock crows, you will deny me three
times." And he went out and wept bitterly.
—Matthew 26:69–75

[Jesus said,] "I am gentle and humble in heart."
—Matthew 11:29

At the fourth station, we find Jesus betrayed once again, this time by his close friend and disciple Peter. Matthew tells us in his Gospel that Peter denies having ever known Jesus: "I do not know what you are talking about," he says to the servant-girl. This is the fisherman from whose boat Jesus once preached to crowds at Lake Gennesaret. This is the disciple who walked briefly on the water beside Jesus. This is the friend who cut off the ear of the soldier taking Jesus away to be crucified. This is the man who said to Christ, "Even though I must die with you, I will not deny you." His betrayal is hard to believe, and then again, it is not.

A shallow sense of self-preservation is always the enemy of humility. Peter was weak, and so are we. How often do we identify ourselves with Jesus as we live out our days, or are we more focused on maintaining whatever image we have of who we are?

When we feel threatened, we are all prone to anger, and Peter's "I do not know the man!" is something we shout inside our souls whenever we brace ourselves to defend against a perceived danger. Perhaps we feel our space is threatened because someone wants the same office as we do at work. Perhaps we feel our time is in danger because we believe that we are long overdue to get a break one Saturday while our spouse watches the kids. Perhaps the "threat" is something as small as someone else's seeming to receive more attention than we do.

Anger of this sort is the antithesis of humility. *Humility* is from the Latin *humilis*, for "lowly, humble," and literally means "on the ground"—from *humus*, "earth." The word *humility* reminds us that we are made from soil, that we will one day die and go back to the soil, and that we are weak creatures, saved by grace, and made to love.

We must take a lesson from Peter. We must sheathe the quick swords of our petty self-interest. Peter's experience in turning his back on Jesus reminds us all that we must be students of humility if we wish our small-minded selfishness to be healed.

THURSDAY MORNING, FIRST WEEK OF LENT

When we look at nothing but ourselves, we leave no room for love. If we schedule our days according to our desires, if we are arrogant about all we have learned, and if we cling adamantly to our opinions, likes, dislikes, and options—we are seeing nothing but ourselves.

God's pilgrims are always found on God's path. To walk this journey, we must relinquish everything we have that is not God; then we will discover that in "having nothing," we possess everything. We navigate by trusting in God through faith; then we will see where to take the next step. Once our cravings are crushed and our souls humbled, we start becoming healed by what we love.

—John of the Cross: *Ascent of Mount Carmel*

We should all try to be like the monk who decided *not* to avoid those people who hurt his feelings or made him uncomfortable. We surely would call this behavior "strange," because who wants to be with people who annoy us or make us feel bad? But the monk decided to live his life according to this odd notion. The more a person hurt his feelings or insulted him, the keener he was to be around them.

His rationale was simple. The monk believed that he could learn the most from those who made his life difficult. Conversely, he felt that people who only said good things to him, complimenting him on his work and life, were the real obstacles. He saw flattery, no matter how "well-deserved," as a lie, a stumbling-block to spiritual growth.

—*Sayings of the Fathers and Mothers*

THURSDAY EVENING, FIRST WEEK OF LENT

The Holy Scripture tells us that any person in love with self-promotion will be brought low, while the modest person will be exalted. The ladder of Jacob, on which God's angels went up and down between heaven and earth, symbolizes the dialogue each one of us needs to have with God. For us, however, every step taken up that ladder in arrogance will bring us down the ladder, and every unassuming step we take down into humility will lift our souls up to God.

Humility is a process, with many stages. First, respect God as love. If we remember this essential truth, it will help us embrace our identity as God's children. Next, relinquish your desire to control everything. Follow the Lord instead; he said, "I have come down from heaven, not to do my own will, but the will of him who sent me." Immaturity is its own punishment, and maturity is a gift in itself.

Then, out of a love for God, respect the authority wherever you are. The Lord himself set us an example in this, as St. Paul said, "He became obedient to the point of death." Next, patiently accept and endure the difficulties that godly obedience requires. As the Psalm says, "Wait for the LORD; be strong, and let your heart take courage; wait for the LORD!" God rewards those who work hard when life is strenuous. They keep St. Paul's words in mind always, "In all these things we are more than conquerors through him who loved us."

Then you must confess your shortcomings to a spiritual guide. Never hide your faults. Accept without complaint unpleasant conditions; see yourself merely as a humble worker for God. Consider yourself lower than others, and do nothing that does not benefit the entire community. To learn how to contribute in this meaningful way, you must be mentored by the wisdom of your elders.

Always listen to others. Never speak unless you absolutely must. Proverbs says, "When words are many, transgression is not lacking." And never laugh at someone else's expense. Speak to each other gently, with kindness and restraint, because the wise are known by the simplicity of their words. Also, your every physical movement should be humble.

Whether you are in church, at prayer, on a journey, in the fields, or anywhere else, you should sit, move, or stand modestly.

The person who clambers up through these stages of humility will arrive at God's love, which casts out all fear. This love becomes then the main focus of that person's life, and they become happy, praying and working for God.

—Benedict: *Rule*

FRIDAY MORNING, FIRST WEEK OF LENT

Sometimes we think obedience is one long climb up a steep, arduous hill. We believe God is nearer to us on a mountaintop than in the low valley, but if the lofty mountain is arrogance, our Lord much prefers the valley of humility. If we are not being humble, we cannot thrive in God. If we wish our heavenly Father to hear us, we must refuse to be rude to others, because almighty God has regard for the profoundly humble. God is with us when we act kindly toward others, wherever we may be. God loves kindness.

That is why, if you love God, you will want to be kind, because God's love is never lazy. We must live out our love for God in how we talk, in how we think, and in how we act. A person must complete God's teachings by working diligently every day on Christlike behavior. Love must be willing to work, or it is not love.

—Ælfric of Eynsham: *Sermons*

FRIDAY EVENING, FIRST WEEK OF LENT

Abba Poemen taught:

Anger moves predictably. First it finds a toehold in our hearts, then we scowl our displeasure at someone, next we lash at them with cruel words, and finally we become violent. Learn to be patient when insulted. Don't let bitterness grow in your heart. If you stop resentment there, anger will not flare up into your face, distorting your features, but if you cannot quite practice that much restraint and do find yourself glaring at someone, at least hold your tongue. When irritated, do not say what you are thinking, and yet, if you cannot stop yourself from speaking harshly, please refuse the next bad idea. Do not be violent. Forget the insult. Move on.

Remember, too, that if someone attacks and wounds you, and you choose to let them go free, forgiving them, you are responding the way Christ does. You have made the right decision. But a person who looks to wound or slander is living like the devil.

Amma Theodora said, "Here's a good response to an insult: 'I could say something equally ugly back to you, but God's teachings shut my mouth.'"

—*Sayings of the Fathers and Mothers*

SATURDAY MORNING, FIRST WEEK OF LENT

Humility is knowing who you are and what flaws you possess. Benedict outlined the steps that lead us to humility. The first one is the most important. Respect God, and look at your neighbors with the truth of agape love, instead of letting your relationship with God be merely abstract. Develop the ability to feel others' pain. When you see someone hungry, feel the pangs of starvation in you. When you see someone sick, consider the difficulties that come with being ill. When you see someone depressed, enter into their anger and their fear and imagine how terrible they must feel. Also, when you see a friend accomplish something good, be happy for them, as if the good thing had happened to you. When you recognize yourself in your neighbor, you can sift through your own experiences and figure out how best to love and appreciate that person. Remember that in the Sermon on the Mount Jesus said, "Blessed are the merciful."

Looking down on us as we climb the ladder of humility, Jesus, the Lord of truth, says: "Come to me, all you that are weary and are carrying heavy burdens, and I will give you rest." Come. This invitation is for everyone. If we go by way of humility, we find rest. What is this rest? Love. It ends the starvation of worrying and gives us the most delicious food. Love revives us when we are tired, strengthens us when we are fragile, helps us count our blessings when we are depressed, lightens our loads, and teaches us kindness. Humility, with its loaf of godly sorrow and cup of repentance, goes well with love. That is why they are always served together.

—Bernard of Clairvaux: *On Humility and Pride*

SATURDAY EVENING, FIRST WEEK OF LENT

The friars asked St. Francis, "What virtue do we most need to be Christ's friend?"

He answered them:

> Poverty is the way to Christ. It triggers humility. Let poverty grow your soul and you will produce many good spiritual fruits. The Gospel calls poverty the "treasure hidden in a field." We are told to sell all we have and buy that field. To know Christlike poverty, stop focusing on how smart you believe you are. The only thing you get if you cling stubbornly to your own opinion is a deadly love affair with yourself. This obduracy is one of the hardest "possessions" to relinquish.
>
> St. Francis also showed them what he meant by opening himself up to every person in need. Though he had but little, Francis gave away anything and everything he had, even altar furnishings, to help those who had nothing.

—Bonaventure: The Life of St. Francis

SECOND SUNDAY MORNING OF LENT

The more a person is humbled, the more that person will be exalted. Look at Jesus. As we read in Philippians, "He humbled himself and became obedient to the point of death—even death on a cross. Therefore God also highly exalted him and gave him the name that is above every name, so that at the name of Jesus every knee should bend."

Water works the same way. The harder you slap water, pressing down on it vigorously, the higher the splash. This principle applies to the javelin throw also. The farther back a person goes before starting their run-up in the javelin throw, the farther they can hurl the javelin.

This is also true with humility. Humility is a lowly nothingness creating the highest something of community, binding us together, as we read in Ephesians, "There is one body and one Spirit, just as you were called to the one hope of your calling, one Lord, one faith, one baptism, one God and Father of all, who is above all and through all and in all."

This is no ordinary love Paul is describing. This concern is altruism, love of the "other" person. We are called to love each other with a uniting love, and the bond between us must be as secure as your arm's connection to your shoulder. Agape love produces the most delicious and nourishing spiritual fruits.

So we ask you, Lord, to illumine our hearts! Because you love us, shine the incandescence of your divine knowledge on our dark eyes. Open them to the true meaning of your gospel. Teach us about agape love. Help us overcome our selfish greed so we can think and live in kindness. Warm us with your love. We praise you and your eternal Father and your life-giving Spirit, forever. Amen.

—John Chrysostom: *Sermons* and *Divine Liturgy*

SECOND SUNDAY EVENING OF LENT

The contemplation of God teaches you that wisdom is hidden in humility. Contemplation is a spiritual exercise best understood if we look at its resemblance to a ladder. What is this tool for? We use ladders for climbing, to reach things we need. In the same way, the soul climbs through the usefulness of contemplation and its mysteries up to divine knowledge, our greatest necessity. David sang about this in the Psalms: "Happy are those whose strength is in you, in whose heart are the highways to Zion. . . . They go from strength to strength." The treasure at the top of the ladder is God. He is the only one who can make us happy.

The wisdom of contemplation is also like a ladder because both have steps that go up and down. Alone in your room, you will find that contemplation provides rungs on which your soul can climb up to God, but it also requires that you humble yourself by taking a few steps down the ladder. In dialogue with God, we learn that "all who exalt themselves will be humbled, and those who humble themselves will be exalted."

And the rungs of this ladder are love.

—John of the Cross: *The Dark Night of the Soul*

Jesus is judged by Pilate

THE GIFT OF GRACE

As soon as it was morning, the chief priests held a consultation with the elders and scribes and the whole council. They bound Jesus, led him away, and handed him over to Pilate. Pilate asked him, "Are you the King of the Jews?" He answered him, "You say so." Then the chief priests accused him of many things. Pilate asked him again, "Have you no answer? See how many charges they bring against you." But Jesus made no further reply, so that Pilate was amazed.
—Mark 15:1–5

All we like sheep have gone astray; we have all turned to our own way, and the LORD has laid on him the iniquity of us all.
—Isaiah 53:6

At the fifth station, we find Jesus betrayed once again, this time by the political system. As a Roman prefect, Pontius Pilate's main concern is making the safest decision. Afraid of offending Emperor Tiberius, afraid of upsetting the people, and afraid of the bitter chief priests, Pilate decrees that an innocent man, Jesus, shall be crucified. Meanwhile, Jesus says nothing. And no one defends him.

Meeting injustice with a quiet strength is grace. Standing before Pilate, Jesus reveals true moral muscle. In doing so, he releases the unmerited, freely given love of God for stubborn, sinful humanity; we call this act grace. *Grace* means "favor, kindness," even "thankfulness," and originates from the Latin *gratia*. What does God's grace look like? It is a blameless, reviled man accepting an undeserved death, for love of others.

We have all been falsely accused at some time. The sting of slander is hard to handle. It is normal to want to react immediately and defend our honor. When someone attacks us verbally, we attack back—or that is what we would like to do. But Christ calls us away from the "normal" path and onto God's. He shows that truth here as he stands silently before Pilate.

This scene with its loud accusers also forms a parable of the destructive power of the tongue. Rumors and lies can kill, as we read in the book of James:

> How great a forest is set ablaze by a small fire! And the tongue is a fire. The tongue is placed among our members as a world of iniquity; it stains the whole body, sets on fire the cycle of nature, and is itself set on fire by hell. For every species of beast and bird, of reptile and sea creature, can be tamed and has been tamed by the human species, but no one can tame the tongue—a restless evil, full of deadly poison.

Shakespeare's Hamlet, trying to discern a way through the murderous lies of the Denmark court, uses sarcasm to condemn the destructive power of the tongue, saying, "Words, words, words."

Jesus as he stands before Pilate is an unforgettable image of life's unfairness. This situation reminds us that Christ understands the pain of defamation better than anyone on earth. It also advises us not to slander anyone, but to defend those who are treated unjustly and stand by those who are alone and hurting. We see that silence sometimes forms the best defense and that God's truth is powerful, even when left unspoken.

We must learn to listen without ceasing to God's eloquent and healing silence. Only then can we have the inner strength to avoid being Pilate ourselves, making expedient decisions instead of the Christlike ones that bring us joy and truth and strength.

MONDAY MORNING, SECOND WEEK OF LENT

During Lent, a monk visited Abba Poemen with some questions that were bothering him. In particular, he wanted to know how to control his tongue. So they talked a while. Then, as the brother rose to leave, he thanked Poemen for his help, and said, "I almost didn't come today."

"Why not?"

"I thought I might disturb your routine of spiritual discipline for Lent."

To which Poemen replied, "God doesn't teach us to close doors of wood, but to shut the door that is our mouth."

—*Sayings of the Fathers and Mothers*

MONDAY EVENING, SECOND WEEK OF LENT

We read in Judges that Manoah, Samson's father, spoke with an angel of the LORD, saying, "What is your name, so that we may honor you when your words come true?"

But the angel of the LORD said to him, "Why do you ask my name? It is too wonderful."

This secret Name transcends all names, becoming, in essence, nameless. On the other hand, Christians give this Name many names, when they say the Unsayable said, "I AM WHO I AM" and "I am the life" and "I am the Light" and "I am God" and "I am the Truth." They celebrate the Creator under many titles taken from this created universe, such as "Good" and "Beautiful" and "Omniscient" and "Beloved" and "God of gods" and "Lord of lords" and "Holy, Holy, Holy" and "Eternal" and "Essential" and "Creator" and "Life-Giver" and "Wisdom" and "Mind" and "Word" and "the One who Knows" and "the Keeper of Spiritual Gold" and "Power" and "Ruler" and "King of kings" and "Ancient of Days" and "the unchanging Foundation" and "Salvation" and "Righteousness" and "Sanctification" and "Redemption" and "an incomparable Magnificence," and also "the still, small voice in the silence"; they also call him Sun, Star, Fire, Water, Wind or Spirit, Dew, Cloud, Rock, and all Creation, yet they also declare that he is nothing that has been created. That is why the omnipotent, transcending Creator must both be nameless and must also take the names of all things.

God, help me articulate the endless honest names of your unutterable, nameless divinity, for you are Truth. Let us praise with songs of peace the holy Peace and one who began all love and united all things, making us yearn for the long silence of your Harmony.

—Pseudo-Dionysius the Areopagite:
On the Divine Names

TUESDAY MORNING, SECOND WEEK OF LENT

Abba Isaac told this story:

When I was young, I lived with old Abba Cronius, who was not entirely well. I thought he would ask me for my help, but he waited on me instead. In spite of his palsied, shaking hands, he brought water to everyone. The same thing happened when I lived with Abba Theodore. He prepared the meal and called us to eat.

Finally, I approached Abba Theodore: "I want to help. Why don't you ask me?" He said nothing.

I asked the elders the same question, so they went to Abba Theodore: "This brother came to help you. Why don't you give him tasks to do?"

Abba Theodore said: "Who am I to give orders? I have nothing to say to this younger brother, but he is welcome to do whatever he sees me doing."

So I began anticipating Abba Theodore's actions and found I had plenty to keep me busy. His life was his pedagogy. He taught by what he did, and he did without explaining. That is how I learned to work in silence.

—*Sayings of the Fathers and Mothers*

TUESDAY EVENING, SECOND WEEK OF LENT

Jesus, wound me with your kindness, and I will be healed by joy. Dying to self for love of you, longing to be one with you, and my soul melting in you, I live. Help me hunger for you, eternal Bread. Let my soul drink you, Fountain of wisdom. Make me starve for you and crave you. Help me seek you, find you, run to you, meditate on you, speak to you, and work for you, in love. Be my confidence, my peace, my help, my wisdom, and my treasure.

Be my silence.

For your presence is my hope. Your light is my refuge. And your love gives my life balance. Amen.

—Bonaventure: *Prayer*

WEDNESDAY MORNING, SECOND WEEK OF LENT

Set aside time to meditate on God's blessings. If you want to live a rich inner life, leave the crowd. Go apart, and be with Jesus. Nobody lives safely in the public eye without first learning to make the most of time alone. Those who have not learned to thrive during periods of obscurity, have egos susceptible to the pressures of the pack when they are out in public. And those who do not love to be silent are more likely to say something foolish when they do speak.

A ruler unwilling to be ruled can never be a good ruler, and a leader who never learned to obey can never be a good leader. Every saint feared God. They knew humility was a necessity, no matter how famous they were for virtues and talents.

Remember—do not be surprised by a constant feeling of insecurity in this life. Only those who are too confident feel a false security. Often people in the public eye are worshipped by crowds, but these celebrities are in grave danger of becoming trapped in self-absorption. Temptations, then, are good for you, because they keep us from feeling too secure and too filled with pride.

So it is much better for you to be unheard of and to cultivate your salvation, than it is for you to neglect your soul and to become a great spiritual leader. Leave vanity to those who are vain. Aim instead for God's goals. Close the door and meet with Jesus, your best Friend. Stay in the quiet of your room with him, and you will discover peace. If you wish to advance as a Christian (I mean spiritually), you must respect God, embrace discipline of your mind and body, and eschew unhealthy diversions such as drunkenness and other things. Sorrow opens the door to many blessings.

So, in the privacy of your room, shut the door and confess your sins to God. Know the grief that comes from becoming acquainted with who you are. In the quiet of your room, get to know yourself again. In that silence, your fumbling soul will grow in virtue as you discover the Bible's hidden truths. When you withdraw from the world's tumult, you will find the space to cry the tears that bind you to our Creator.

—Thomas à Kempis: *Imitation of Christ*

WEDNESDAY EVENING, SECOND WEEK OF LENT

Abba Macarius was asked how to pray, and he said:

Lift your hands to heaven and ask, "Forgive me, Lord." If you are still anxious, pray, "Help me." You really don't need to say much. God knows our needs. His mercy is never tardy.

A man asked Abba Poemen how he should live when he got back home, and the Abba said: "When you return home, be as vigilant about what you say as if you were a stranger in your own town. Do not seek attention. Do not work at getting others to agree with you. Do not hope to become influential or powerful. This humility will bring you great peace of mind."

Syncletica said: "We need humility the way ships need nails."

—*Sayings of the Fathers and Mothers*

Jesus is scourged and crowned with thorns

THE DARKNESS OF SUFFERING AND ITS MEANING

Then Pilate took Jesus and had him flogged.
And the soldiers wove a crown of thorns and
put it on his head, and they dressed him in
a purple robe. They kept coming up to him,
saying, "Hail, King of the Jews!" and striking
him on the face.
—John 19:1–3

To the Lord our God belong mercy and
forgiveness, for we have rebelled against
him, and have not obeyed the voice of the
LORD our God by following his laws, which he
set before us by his servants the prophets.
—Daniel 9:9–10

At the sixth station, we find Jesus being flogged and then painfully humiliated with the crown of thorns. The Gospel writers describe this terrible torture with compelling terseness. They do not elaborate. There is no need.

Flogging alone could kill a man. The whips are made by tying sharp objects like sheep bones to the ends of leather thongs and attaching these lashes to a wooden handle. The naked man is then tied to a post or in some other way is tightly bound so that he cannot move, and then he is attacked with this deadly whip in an orderly fashion, stripe beside stripe beside stripe, by soldiers who carry out scourgings as their profession. Jesus endures dozens of these lacerating lashes. And he is spat on and cursed.

In the darkness of suffering, we learn the limits of our bodies and our souls, and we search the pain for meaning. When we do, we can remember that Jesus endures his physical and psychological torture with patience, and with his help, so can we. We can take comfort from the suffering of Christ, because his anguish shows us that God is in our every hardship. This mystery is the heart of God's love.

We are also reminded that torture continues today, everywhere in the world, in wars and even in families as abuse, and only forgiveness can break the chain of one injured person inflicting pain on another. In persecution, in sickness, in hunger, in discrimination, in poverty, in uncertainty, and in heartache, Christ is with us, always, in every moment of our darkness. His presence with us makes our suffering incalculably valuable.

Because Christ is intimate with the darkness of pain and death, accepting them completely, he has transformed this darkness into what Pseudo-Dionysius the Areopagite calls the "secret hiding place" of God, and "an excess of his divine Light."

THURSDAY MORNING, SECOND WEEK OF LENT

A brother said to Abba Macarius, "Teach me something that will help my soul."

Macarius said, "Go to the cemetery and yell insults at the dead." Confused, the brother went to the tombs anyway. He threw rocks at the graves and screamed abuse at the dead.

When he returned, his teacher asked him, "Did the dead notice what you did?"

"No."

Then Macarius said, "Go back. Praise them this time."

Even more confused, the brother went back to the cemetery and told the dead they had lived exemplary lives. He called them apostles, bragged on them as saints.

When he returned, Macarius asked him, "What did they say this time?"

"Nothing."

Macarius said then:

"You mean—first you offended them with cruel insults, next you flattered them with effusive compliments, but they never said a word? Take note of this. If you really want salvation, you must be like them. Ignore wrongs done to you, and think nothing of praises you receive. Be like the dead. Then you'll taste salvation."

—*Sayings of the Fathers and Mothers*

THURSDAY EVENING, SECOND WEEK OF LENT

Three-in-One God, let your incandescent darkness amaze us. Take us beyond knowledge. Show us the heights of mystical wisdom. Let your divine silence speak, and we will see the simple and absolute permanence of you. We'll hear the harmony of your changeless Truth. This is your beauty. Guide us to your invisible spirit, so we can experience oneness with you. We pray to know you better.

To experience this union with God, abandon your five senses and also abandon thinking. If you want to know oneness with the God of love, who cannot be quantified or labeled or categorized, forget yourself and everything in your world. If you hunger to meet God, remember he made darkness his secret hiding place. Work to be pure, because purity is irresistible, happy, freeing. Then you'll experience the joy of the darkness that is an excess of his divine Light.

Do not bother trying to explain this to people who believe that with their brains alone they can reach God. Their God is one-dimensional. Flat. Contemplating God teaches us that theology is both huge and minute, infinite and detailed. It shows us that the gospel is deep and wide, and also narrow; that God is eloquent and reticent, and sometimes mute. God is found where opposites rub together. We pass through the wisest voices and the brightest visions and climb the highest spiritual hills, to reach the darkness that is, above all, a superabundance of Light, and God's home.

To enter this divine darkness, we must be unafraid to let go of our understanding and be truly still in every sense of that word, *still*. Empty out your talents and abilities and be quiet before God. This emptiness is real sight and real knowledge. Released from seeing and knowing, we go beyond sight and knowledge, becoming one with the mystery of the all-knowing God. United with him, we gain a knowledge of something that is beyond our understanding. We see the darkness that is too much Light.

We must remove everything that keeps us from praising him. We can do this the same way that a sculptor carves a statue from stone. Looking at the stone, the artist sees a beautiful shape in it, and then removes everything from the stone that is *not* that image. We must sculpt everything in our minds that is not God, to reveal the divine beauty hidden in our souls. Doing this, we enter the radiant darkness that, concealed by the light of created things, shines more brightly than they.

This experience is impossible to describe. Thinking is wingless, and language cannot follow where your spirit can fly. Let go, and allow the everlasting "Yes" to speak to you. Touch Love's limitlessness. Dialogue with the Word. Become friends with the Mystery who loves us.

—Pseudo-Dionysius the Areopagite:
The Mystical Theology

FRIDAY MORNING, SECOND WEEK OF LENT

At first, as you walk down the path of intimacy with God, your struggles will be intense and painful, but once you pass through these, you will feel unending joy. Working to grow closer to God is not unlike trying to start a fire in the desert. You light the fire, your eyes sting, smoke clogs your throat, and you begin choking.

This is so like what happens when we try to light the "consuming fire" of God within. See how similar they are? Accept the difficulty of your task. Work hard, and know that tears will surely come.

—Pseudo-Athanasius: *Life of Syncletica*

A Desert Father told his brothers that spiritual discipline is hard work, but has significant rewards— one benefit is that we learn to accept adversity better. He said problems and their pain are not unlike dogs and their ability to bite:

People who reject pain, refusing to deal with life, will find that every difficulty throws them off-balance. Hard times and dogs have something in common: Dogs bite people they don't know, but wag their tails when they see people they recognize. Problems are like that. To the inexperienced, they bring bitter pain, but to those who have disciplined themselves to accept trouble and deal with it, they are kindly disposed. We must all bear the adversities of life and learn to turn them into joy.

—*Sayings of the Fathers and Mothers*

FRIDAY EVENING, SECOND WEEK OF LENT

Halfway through my journey, I got lost in the darkest forest. I was alone and scared. I don't know how it happened. All of a sudden, I was off the path. Walking down a hill and through a valley, I was dejected, deeply regretful. Looking up, I saw the brightest sun on the best of roads, and so I rested before beginning to climb a mountain. As I started up the road, a lion blocked my way. Then a wolf appeared, baring her teeth, followed by a leopard. These hungry beasts terrified me, and I went back down, abandoning all hope of climbing up.

Suddenly I saw someone or something approaching me. It was the great poet Virgil who sang of Troy. He came to help me, saying:

You're afraid. Fear is a burden and a distraction. If you let it, it can stop you from accepting the challenges of adversity. Don't you want to climb the Mountain of Joy? Then don't fear mere shadows. Follow me. You must take a different path.

Later, Beatrice, my guide, her eyes as sparkling as stars, challenged me in her angelic voice: "Why do you fear what can't hurt you? Why be scared? Why let risk upset you?"

These words finally set me free. Even though I was still exhausted and worried, I took the energy I had left, and with it tried to imitate the smallest, most unnoticed flowers that stand up straight when the sun shines down on them, leaving the chilly darkness of night behind, rising up and opening in the life-giving light. With my newfound courage, I took my first step along the strangest, most profound path, which ultimately led to Paradise.

This vision convinced me how small language is. I also realized that no one who has ever seen this Light can reject it for a lesser brightness. God's Sun is the good of everything I need. He turns my will like a wheel in the Love that moves the sun and every one of the stars. There in this vision my mind rested in the Light of eternity, completely content

in reaching its intent—God. And I was still, filled
with joy through looking.

—Dante Alighieri: *The Divine Comedy*

SATURDAY MORNING, SECOND WEEK OF LENT

Abba Arsenius often said,

If you place an unbaked brick, still moist to the
touch, in the foundation of a building, it won't
support the structure. But if you bake it first until that
brick is rock-hard, it makes a splendid support for
that foundation. This is why you must be thankful for
trouble when it comes your way. The fires of trouble's
furnace make your soul firm, strong, unmoved.

When asked, "How can we learn not to be easily
offended?" a Desert Father said:

Consider how dogs hunt rabbits. One dog spots
the rabbit and runs after it, giving chase. When the
other dogs in the pack see that one dog race down
that path, they take off after him, until they become
winded and quit, never having seen the rabbit. So
they turn back. That one dog, however, will pursue
his quarry until he catches it. He ignores briers, rocks,

injury, and weariness. He takes no notice that he is alone. He will not rest until he has caught that rabbit. It is the same with those who seek Christ, training their eyes on the cross. They ignore what upsets or injures them. Their eyes are fixed on reaching God's love.

—*Sayings of the Fathers and Mothers*

SATURDAY EVENING, SECOND WEEK OF LENT

Do not forget that sin is an obstacle. Remember Abraham's words to the rich man in hell: "Between you and us a great chasm has been fixed." This verse in the Gospel of Luke is saying that sin is an impenetrable wall or black shadow in our souls, a "chasm" preventing us from communing with Jesus. So lift up your lamp.

Look and see that this shadow has five windows, through which sin comes into our souls. As the prophet Jeremiah said, "Death has come up into our windows." These "windows" are the five senses through which the soul exits to follow perverse pleasures and feed on earthly things, contrary to the dignity of our natures. When the soul is curious, it eyes the glittering vanities of this world, and then runs after them.

It hears about the latest exciting news, and rushes after it, and so on. These empty pursuits keep us from enjoying the sweetness of our inner spiritual senses. Board up these windows. Open them only when absolutely needed.

Closing the windows of your spirit against sin would not be hard to do, if just once you could see your soul as it really is. If you could glimpse how beautiful you are, shutting your windows against sin would be easy. Remember this. Even under the black cloak of sin, your soul is still beautiful. Do not abandon reason and become like a beast. Do not neglect your soul. Do not scavenge for food in the wilderness of the world. It simply is not nourishing. If you are going to be a beggar, turn to our Lord Jesus. He has everything you need.

—Walter Hilton: *Scale of Perfection*

THIRD SUNDAY MORNING OF LENT

If you could calm your body's loud demands—if you could blind your point of view; if you could silence noise and dreams and language and symbols and everything that does not last forever—if your soul could be quiet with itself; if you could relinquish analysis—if you could lose your anxious self-consciousness; if you could listen only to your Maker speak, not through anything but himself: then we would hear Being, the unmoving Wisdom. And if we could sustain this not-thinking for any length of time, it would swallow us up into unspeakable delights of the soul, and we would know what Jesus meant when he told the parable of the talents, giving this invitation: "Enter into the joy of your master."

I was commanded to practice being still before God, and with his help, I did. I entered the dim recesses of my being and saw there, with my sober eye, above my turbulent self, the unchanging Light. This Light was not above my soul as oil floats above water or as heaven is found above the earth. This Light was above my soul because it is the Light who made me. If you know the Truth, you know this eternal Light, who is Love. Then a voice on high said to me, "Be mature, and feed on me. When you nourish yourself with me, you will not transform me the way you transform your ordinary food into your body when you eat. Feast on me, and you are transformed into me."

—Augustine: *Confessions*

THIRD SUNDAY EVENING OF LENT

As gold is heated in many furnaces, one after another, so that any impurity not separated out in the first furnace can be separated out in the second, and so on, until all remaining impurities are removed in the final smelting, I watched my younger sister, the nun Macrina, as her soul was refined by grief. She knew many earthly losses until her heart became absolutely pure. Like the best athletes, she persevered. She never let difficulties break her spirit. Macrina worked at her faith.

For example, she grieved when our brother Basil, the Bishop of Caesarea, died in AD 379. The whole world—even God's enemies—mourned our brother as a Christian leader known for integrity and kindness. When the news reached the remote location where Macrina lived, sorrow overwhelmed her. This heartache and others tested her.

Later, as Macrina lay dying, I went to visit her. Even then she was tranquil. When she saw me at the door, she raised herself up on an elbow in greeting. Even though she was dying, she was thankful, praying to God: "I'm grateful for this gift from you. You knew that I, your servant, wanted this visit with Gregory." Macrina tried to hide her pain from me by being cheerful and making pleasant conversation, but at times it was hard for her to breathe.

Eventually, we talked of Basil's death, and my grief showed in my face, but Macrina began discussing God's secret divine ways, as revealed in human disasters, like death. I felt the Holy Spirit with us as she talked. I was comforted. Her words lifted my soul away from this earth, and I was allowed to live, for a moment, in heaven.

—Gregory of Nyssa: *Life of Macrina*

Jesus carries his cross

THE BEAUTY OF ENDURANCE

When the chief priests and the police saw him, they shouted, "Crucify him! Crucify him!" Pilate said to them, "Take him yourselves and crucify him; I find no case against him." . . . They cried out, "Away with him! Away with him! Crucify him!" Pilate asked them, "Shall I crucify your King?" The chief priests answered, "We have no king but the emperor." Then he handed him over to them to be crucified. So they took Jesus; and carrying the cross by himself, he went out to what is called The Place of the Skull, which in Hebrew is called Golgotha.
—John 19:6, 15–17

He called the crowd with his disciples, and said to them, "If any want to become my followers, let them deny themselves and take up their cross and follow me."
—Mark 8:34

At the seventh station, Jesus still does not give up. Weary and battered to the point of death, he picks up his heavy cross and begins walking to Golgotha. The crossbar that Jesus carries weighs about one hundred pounds. Considering his flogging and loss of blood, his endurance is remarkable. It shows that he loves us and meets us where we pick up our own crosses and follow him.

Endure means "to continue forever," from *durare* ("to last") and *in-* ("thoroughly"). We may wonder how Jesus perseveres here, until we contemplate the truth of Teresa of Avila's words in the *Interior Castle*, "I know the power obedience has of making things possible that seem hopeless." *Obedience* is another helpful word. It means "to listen to," from *audire* ("to hear"). If we follow Jesus in obeying God, we will listen for our Lord's words of encouragement and be strengthened to pick up our crosses and move forward into the mystery of love, experiencing for ourselves the beauty of persevering in Christ.

MONDAY MORNING, THIRD WEEK OF LENT

Joy and eternal praise be to you, Lord Jesus Christ. Your gorgeous forehead never turned away from what was right and true. Blessed be your forehead! May all creatures praise it. Amen.

Your bright, compassionate eyes look kindly on all who ask you for grace and mercy, in love. Blessed be your eyes, eyelids, and wonderful eyebrows! May your lovely, kind vision be praised forever. Amen.

Your sympathetic ears listen gladly to everyone who speaks humbly. Blessed be Your ears. May they always be filled with good words. Amen.

Your very clean teeth chewed physical food sensibly for the nourishing of your holy body. May your teeth be blessed and honored by every creature. Amen.

You never used your tongue poorly, and you never kept quiet except honestly and helpfully. You always said whatever God wanted you to say. Blessed be your tongue. Amen.

My Lord Jesus Christ, blessed be your throat, stomach, and intestines. May all your sacred internal workings be honored because they fed you well and kept your precious body functioning efficiently. They nourished your bodily life for the redemption of souls, and to the angels' joy. Amen.

You, Lord, are our leader because on your sacred shoulders and neck you carried the weight of the cross before you smashed the gates of hell forever. Blessed be your neck and shoulders for enduring this great burden. Amen.

—Birgitta of Sweden: *Prayers*

MONDAY EVENING, THIRD WEEK OF LENT

Our Father in heaven, hallowed be your name. Your kingdom come. Your will be done, on earth as it is in heaven. Give us this day our daily bread. And forgive us our debts, as we also have forgiven our debtors. And do not bring us to the time of trial, but rescue us from the evil one.

—Matthew 6:9–13

I believe in God the Father Almighty, maker of heaven and earth; and in Jesus Christ his only Son our Lord: who was conceived by the Holy Spirit, born of the Virgin Mary, suffered under Pontius Pilate, was crucified, dead, and buried; the third day he rose from the dead; he ascended into heaven, and sitteth at the right hand of God the Father Almighty; from thence he shall come to judge the quick and the dead. I believe in the Holy Spirit, the holy catholic church, the communion of saints, the forgiveness of sins, the resurrection of the body, and the life everlasting. Amen.

—*The Apostles' Creed*

Let us read the Lord's Prayer and the Apostles' Creed together and look at them closely. Why do we have these? The Lord's Prayer is easy to memorize, and saying it helps lighten the burden of sin that we all carry. The Apostles' Creed helps us call on the Lord and be saved. It answers the question St. Paul asked in his letter to the Romans; after St. Paul reflected on the prophet Joel's teaching on grace—that "everyone who calls on the name of the LORD shall be saved" —he then asked, "But how are they to call on one in whom they have not believed?" We desperately need God's mercy, since each of us knows the pain of failure. The Apostles' Creed helps us turn to God in a crisis.

Together, these two positive prayers strengthen our spiritual muscles, which are faith, hope, and love.

Faith is the first to believe, as hope and love pray; then faith prays because without faith, having hope and loving are not possible. Remember that love is never found without hope, that hope is never found without love, and that faith is always found with hope and love.

—Augustine: *Handbook on Faith, Hope, and Love*

TUESDAY MORNING, THIRD WEEK OF LENT

God says,

Consider my Son, the gentle, loving Word born in a stable while Mary was on a journey. What does he show you? True pilgrims are constantly being born anew in the stable of self-knowledge. There by grace you will find Christ born within your soul. Look at baby Jesus lying there between the animals. He was so poor. Mary had nothing to cover him with, and it was winter. The breath of animals and a blanket of hay kept him warm. Look again. This baby is the fire of Love, but he chose to endure the bitterest cold in his humanity.

The whole time my Son lived on earth, he chose to endure suffering.

Sweet measureless love, who moved you? Love alone. O gentlest love, Jesus! To strengthen each person's soul and free it from the weaknesses of disobedience, you built a wall around it, mixing the flow of your own blood into the lime for the mortar. This blood fuses the soul with God's gentle divine will and fits it for his love, because just as lime mixed with water is put between stone and stone to bind them together securely, so God mixed the blood of his only-begotten Son into the living lime, the fire of God's shining love.

God put this celestial cement between himself and every one of his creatures—because there is no blood without fire, nor fire without blood.

—Catherine of Siena: *Dialogue* and *Letters*

TUESDAY EVENING, THIRD WEEK OF LENT

Dearest Jesus, I have chosen you above all others. You are the most trustworthy lover of my soul, the best partner of my life. My rational soul pines for you. I offer my heart to you. I choose you as my companion and guide. I offer you myself—body and soul—as your servant. I belong to you, and you to me.

Cement me to you, my true Love. Your love and beauty attract me to you. You are gentle, and when I obey you, I bind myself to you. Clinging to you, I understand what love is. Your kindness draws me to you, and I want to be with you.

Christ says in response,

I will support you through my Holy Spirit. I will draw you close to me in inseparable union. You will be my guest. I will embrace you, cherish you, make you an enduring robe of the finest purple from my precious blood. I will complete your desire for me, making you forever glad.

—Gertrude the Great: *Spiritual Exercises*

WEDNESDAY MORNING, THIRD WEEK OF LENT

When we persist in compassion, and are aware, sensitive, and open, that is love. God commands us to love, and when we do, he pays us in kindness. The love we experience on earth for God, ourselves, and others is merely an introduction. We will get the full text in heaven. Love is also wisdom. When you love the Lord your God with all your heart, soul, mind, and strength, your loving teaches you what to do next and how to act. The Holy Spirit becomes your guide.

"Love your neighbor as yourself" includes loving your enemies. It is one thing to love someone who loves you in return, but another thing to love someone who resents you. In the first instance, you love the person for who she is. In the second, you love the person for who she can become. Remember that Jesus said: "Do good to those who hate you." Those who are unlovable need the most love. We love them so they may learn of love. We must endure in love, always remembering that God is with us: "His intention toward me was love."

—Bernard of Clairvaux: *Sermon*

WEDNESDAY EVENING, THIRD WEEK OF LENT

Many people think love is best expressed in eloquent words, but love is meant to be a muscle. Love is best put into actions, not words. Love is a relationship between two people who care about each other. Love is also a dialogue rather than a monologue. Love is a sharing, not a selfish acquisition. Because I love you, I want to give you what you need, if I have it, and because you love me, you want to give me what I need, if you have it. That is love.

Learn this way of praying, and your ability to love will be strengthened. First thank God that you can stand before him, with the Holy Spirit as your translator. Then ask God to help you understand in your soul every blessing you have received, and you will possess gratitude and be able to serve God fully. Then contemplate God's acts of creation and redemption. Thank him for these and for sharing his love with you. See that God made our world and animates it still; his sunbeams cover the earth literally, and he also shines his blessings on us—mercy, love, forgiveness, and undying loyalty.

If you follow these spiritual exercises, you will discover that just as the body needs the exercise of walking and running to be strong and to build stamina, the soul needs the exercises of praying and contemplating in Christ, in order to lose its flaccid, exaggerated sense of self and to add invisible sinew.

—Ignatius of Loyola: *Spiritual Exercises*

Jesus is helped by Simon of Cyrene

THE NECESSITY OF FRIENDSHIP

They compelled a passer-by, who was coming
in from the country, to carry his cross; it was
Simon of Cyrene, the father of Alexander
and Rufus.
—Mark 15:21

Is it nothing to you, all you who pass
by? Look and see if there is any sorrow like
my sorrow, which was brought upon me.
—Lamentations 1:12

At the eighth station, Jesus himself needs help. Beaten
and harassed, Christ can carry the terrible weight of
that cross no further. Surely this truth is astonishing.
His burden falls to the ground, and Simon of Cyrene,
who has come into town only to find himself at this
march of death, is compelled to carry Christ's cross.

This event shows us two strong truths. We see
that God himself, as man, reaches the limit of his
endurance, and he must accept and be grateful for
the kindness of a stranger. This story demonstrates

the limitations of our usual definitions of "friendship." We love those who love us back, but Christ demands more: he wants us to consider everyone our neighbor and friend, and their burdens our own—and he leads us by example in this.

First, we see that Christ has, for love of us, surrendered his divinity, embracing pain, and that that submission is how he has come to the end of his earthly strength. Second, we see Simon's act of helping Jesus as a reminder that when we do something kind for a stranger, we are helping Jesus, too, as the Gospel of Matthew records Christ's words:

> I was hungry and you gave me food, I was thirsty and you gave me something to drink, I was a stranger and you welcomed me, I was naked and you gave me clothing, I was sick and you took care of me, I was in prison and you visited me. . . . Truly I tell you, just as you did it to one of the least of these who are members of my family, you did it to me.

We understand that friendship is infinitely more than exchanging cards at Christmas or on a birthday. It is putting myself in someone else's place and trying to see the world from that person's perspective. Friendship is also bearing others' burdens, not because we always feel like it, nor because we expect something in return, but because it is the way of Jesus, who is love incarnate. In the devotionals of this station, we see Christ's willingness to carry our pain to his utmost limit, and we remember that if we are to bear others' problems well, we must first cultivate our deep yearning to be friends with God.

May we learn to listen to our best friend, Christ.

THURSDAY MORNING, THIRD WEEK OF LENT

One of the fathers in the desert said this about love:

We're asked to carry each other's burdens. God wants us to look at those near us, whoever they are, and identify their loads. God requires us to feel compassion and to help others with their difficulties. How? Put your soul in the place of your neighbor's. Become, for a moment, two people in one. Pretend that this is possible. Be a double person. Suffer your neighbor's troubles. Imagine that your neighbor's life is yours. Let tears come, and grieve for and listen to your neighbor. Act as if you have put on your neighbor's actual body. Imagine that you are wearing her face and soul and burdens. Suffer for your neighbor as you would for your own self. Remember that the Bible says, "We are all one body."

—*Sayings of the Fathers and Mothers*

THURSDAY EVENING, THIRD WEEK OF LENT

When I was living in the desert, I went with my good friend Germanus to see Abba Moses, because he had a reputation for giving the best advice on contemplation. I was anxious to get a wise word from him. My heart was burdened and needed good counsel. So, Germanus and I went to Abba Moses with our burdens. We knew he would not offer us advice unless we were earnest in our desire to understand God better, but, as he listened, he saw our tears and knew that our questions were genuine.

Abba Moses shared his wisdom with us. He said that every worldly pursuit has some goal and that the conscientious person will endure any amount of pain and danger to reach that goal. He gave us examples. The farmer braves the scorching sun and deadly cold to plow the earth, because his goal is breaking up the packed soil into the finest sand, clearing out the thorny underbrush, pulling out the weeds, and planting the seed in the best prepared soil, to reap the biggest harvest. Also, a merchant does not waste his day worrying about the uncertainties of trade. He has no time to fear risks, because he is working conscientiously to ensure the success of his business. And those in the military avoid dwelling on the danger of their work, focusing instead on working diligently.

Abba Moses also said that we should work with joy and not complain. When we work cheerfully, he said, an absence of food will not make fasting unattractive, worshipping God daily will not be tiring, reading and meditating on Scripture will not bore us, and the self-deprivation of a life in the desert will not be frightening.

Abba Moses asked us, "What is your goal? Why do you cheerfully endure such hardships for God?"

We said, "For the kingdom of heaven."

He commended us for speaking well, but said we had named an end result, and that he wished to know our immediate goal. So he reformed the question, asking us, "What can you embrace now that will help you reach that ultimate goal?"

We had no answer. Abba Moses told us to clarify this immediate aim for ourselves, because we must not exhaust ourselves for no good reason, or we would be like the person traveling in the wrong direction, who has all the hassle of a journey without the good of arriving at the ultimate destination.

Again, we had no answer, so we waited for him to finish:

"Your immediate goal is a pure heart. Without that, you can never reach the ultimate goal. Fix your eyes on purity. It will keep you on course. Then, if your thoughts wander, look at integrity, and you will find your way back to God's path."

—John Cassian: *Conferences*

FRIDAY MORNING, THIRD WEEK OF LENT

Every time the Lord shared his wisdom with me, my soul gained a good deal, and some visions helped me even more than others. Let me give you an example. My vision of Christ left me with an impression of his extraordinary beauty, which in turn helped me with a serious problem I had been having. Before, my obsessive mind had prevented me from developing my intimacy with Christ. Instead, if I saw that somebody liked me and if I happened to be attracted to him, too, I became inordinately fond of this person. I could not stop thinking about him, though I meant

God no harm. I simply could not stop my mind from wandering to thoughts of this person, constantly. I would so love seeing him and thinking of him and considering all of his good qualities. This tendency became a serious burden. It began to ruin my soul. But after I had seen my Lord's incomparable beauty in my vision, I could no longer find anyone who seemed handsome to me by comparison. So after that, no one else could occupy my thoughts like God.

Today I only have to turn my mind on this vision of the Lord that I carry permanently in my soul, and I become entirely free from this burden.

—Teresa of Avila: *Life*

FRIDAY EVENING, THIRD WEEK OF LENT

The Holy Spirit is the Forgiver, and the Father is the Creator; but only Christ embraced humanity. Of the Trinity, only Christ possessed our human nature. That is why our Savior was weary, which is a miracle. Through his Son, the heavenly Father made creation without becoming tired, but, still, Christ became weary because he assumed the burdens of being a man. His weakness became our strength, because while his divine strength created us, his becoming human redeemed us. Even though Christ alone took on the nature of humanity and suffered for us, we are confident that the whole Trinity in true oneness accomplishes each of these works for us, because they all work one work, always. So we humbly ask the almighty Father, our Creator, to blot out our sins through the Holy Spirit and to protect us from Satan so we may grow in Christ's love.

—Ælfric of Eynsham: *Sermons*

SATURDAY MORNING, THIRD WEEK OF LENT

I saw the profuse bleeding of our Lord's head. Great drops of blood fell from beneath the thorny crown like pellets. These balls of blood were a brownish red and looked like they came from the veins. The blood was very thick and became bright red as it spread.

As the bleeding continued, I saw and understood many things. There was so much blood that it was like drops of water falling from the eaves of a house after a summer rain shower, falling so thick no human brain can count the drops.

What this vision most taught me was that our good Lord—so absolutely to be revered—makes himself familiar and kind to us. This intimacy made my soul joyful and confident.

—Julian of Norwich: *Revelations*

SATURDAY EVENING, THIRD WEEK OF LENT

Christ chose to have parents who were financially poor but morally good; otherwise, people might have admired his elite background and money rather than the deep truths he wanted to teach: "For God's foolishness is wiser than human wisdom, and God's weakness is stronger than human strength." Christ chose a life of poverty to show us that we must absolutely reject riches. He chose not to focus on accumulating things and status, but rather on connecting with people. He chose an ordinary life.

His choices remind us that we must never lust after the world's honors, wealth, power, prestige, and promotion. For his ministry, Christ chose everything that the world considers insignificant—a peasant mother, birth in a stable, life as a carpenter, and fishermen.

Christ's way is through the mundane. He worked, felt hunger pangs, became thirsty, and knew the reality of pain, choosing the day-to-day discipline of a life of virtue over greed and temptation. To encourage us to take up our burdens and follow him into virtue, Christ also died the most painful, shameful death on the cross, choosing not to abandon the truth. Peter said so: "For to this you have been called, because Christ also suffered for you, leaving you an example, so that you should follow in his steps." Christ let himself be subject to rejection and condemnation to death by the great leaders of this world to demonstrate beyond argument that his miracles and teachings are not authorized by an earthly power but by a divine one.

Christ's ministry focused on ordinary people. He made friends with those whom the world sees as unimportant or ugly, and he chose things the world views as nothing special—working with wood, riding a donkey, eating the food of peasants. In the eyes of the world, his teaching seems unremarkable. His approach was necessary for human redemption, because we have much to learn about self-reliance. We have false ideas about trusting ourselves; we are often ignorant and overconfident. We must learn that only God is completely trustworthy and wise. As St. Paul said, "For the message about the cross is foolishness to those who are perishing, but to us who are being saved it is the power of God."

—Thomas Aquinas: *Reasons for the Faith*

FOURTH SUNDAY MORNING OF LENT

Choose the love of Christ over everything that the world can offer. Never let yourself forget that the Lord is our kindest friend, and he works beside us, helping us be more disciplined and less anxious. God is our partner, for, as St. Paul says in his letter to the Romans, the Lord stands beside those who work for his good. To continue on this path with Christ, we should also reflect on these words from St. Paul: "I die every day!" We can focus on doing God's work only if we live each day as if it were our final one on earth. That should not be difficult, because the only certainty we have is life's unpredictability. God alone gives us each new day. See every dawn as the beginning of your final twenty-four hours, and you will never be distracted by the noise and flash of this world. This approach is how you can prevent yourself from growing too attached to money, pleasures of the body, resentment, awards, and worrying.

Work hard, and do not think goodness is impossible for you. Do not dismiss it as something strange and above the realm of your experience. We can all please God. We must only choose well. Many go abroad to study, pursuing knowledge far from home, but the kingdom of God is always here and now, wherever you are, within you. Precisely because the kingdom of God is within, and God is our friend, our salvation only requires that we be willing.

—Athanasius of Alexandria: *The Life of St. Anthony*

FOURTH SUNDAY EVENING OF LENT

O merciful God in Christ Jesus, I beg you, out of your deep love for us, which you have made known to me in my inner person, call us all in you, to you.

God is our friend, and we can deepen our friendship with him through repentance. I wrote this book to prove that point. These words are intended for anyone earnest about redemption, as Matthew's

Gospel says, "For what will it profit them if they gain the whole world but forfeit their life?" If you decide to experience repentance, you must pray, and to pray with authenticity, you must first examine the state of your soul. You will see horrible truths there—that you pay no attention to God, that you are faithless, that you are focused on temporary pleasures. You will see how you are preoccupied, even obsessed, with the shallow, fragile, impermanent things and ways of this short earthly life. You have forgotten to love God and your neighbor. Your steps are not aligned with God's. You spend your days lusting after ungodly behavior. Remember that money cannot gain you entry into heaven. All die. Each of us will know that last breath. Remember this—there is an end.

That is why we must grieve for our sins and long for God's mercy. We were made to work in Christ's vineyard, not to wither and be fruitless branches. So, when you feel godly sorrow, let it work its way through you. Open your heart to it. This sorrow is Christ's powerful Spirit. Its medicine heals your heart and makes you teachable, which is humility. Humility, in turn, has a strong grasp on the words of Christ who loved us so much that he died for us.

This humility will help you live like Christ. It will keep you close to him, until that last breath. May God's eternal goodness and mercy bless you.

—Jacob Boehme: *The Way to Christ*

Jesus meets the women of Jerusalem

THE KNOWLEDGE OF GODLY SORROW

A great number of the people followed him, and among them were women who were beating their breasts and wailing for him. But Jesus turned to them and said, "Daughters of Jerusalem, do not weep for me, but weep for yourselves and for your children. For the days are surely coming when they will say, 'Blessed are the barren, and the wombs that never bore, and the breasts that never nursed.' Then they will begin to say to the mountains, 'Fall on us'; and to the hills, 'Cover us.' For if they do this when the wood is green, what will happen when it is dry?"

—Luke 23:27–31

Cast your burden on the LORD, and he will sustain you; he will never permit the righteous to be moved.

—Psalm 55:22

At the ninth station, Jesus shows the depth of his character as he turns his attention away from his own grief to comfort and to offer words of wisdom to the grieving women of Jerusalem. Throughout his ministry, Christ pays special attention to those on the margins of society; among those disregarded at that time were women. Here, even in his pain, and facing certain death on the cross, he is concerned to dialogue with those in pain, showing the deep respect he has for women, an esteem that he must have acquired in his friendship with his own mother, Mary.

Christ's words, however, are puzzling, until we realize that he is trying to teach these sorrowful women something. They empathize with the tragic suffering of Mary's son, who is bloody and exhausted, but Jesus wants to shift their awareness to the spiritual level, so he says to them in their sadness, "Do not weep for me, but weep for yourselves and for your children."

What can he mean by this command? He is asking them to pray for the gift of godly sorrow. This knowledge was God's greatest gift to David. After David committed adultery with Bathsheba and murdered her husband, Uriah, by proxy, the prophet Nathan confronted him about his sin. David's response in Psalm 51 represents the ultimate example of the spiritual necessity we call godly sorrow:

> Have mercy on me, O God, according to your steadfast love; according to your abundant mercy blot out my transgressions. Wash me thoroughly from my iniquity, and cleanse me from my sin. For I know my transgressions, and my sin is ever before me. Against you, you alone, have I sinned, and done what is evil in your sight, so that you are justified in your sentence and blameless when you pass judgment. Indeed, I was born guilty, a sinner when my mother conceived me. You desire truth in the inward being; therefore teach me wisdom in my secret heart. Purge me with hyssop, and I shall be clean; wash me, and I shall be whiter than snow. Let me hear joy and gladness; let the bones that you have crushed rejoice. Hide your face from my sins, and blot out all my iniquities. Create in me a clean heart, O God, and put a new and right spirit within me. Do not cast me away from your presence, and do not take your holy spirit from me. Restore to me the joy of your salvation, and sustain in me a willing spirit.

MONDAY MORNING, FOURTH WEEK OF LENT

God said,

Dear child, I have shown you that no guilt on earth can be atoned by experiencing suffering simply as pain to be endured. Only when suffering is accepted with longing, love, and heartfelt contrition does it have meaning. The value is not in the suffering, but in the soul's God-focused desire while suffering. This desire and all other virtues possess value and life solely through my only-begotten Son—Christ crucified—because his surrender is the power of your love. Through virtue, the soul can follow his sacrificial footsteps. This surrendering in Christ is the only way suffering has value in reconciling the soul to me.

This reconciliation is accomplished through a gentle, unifying love born from the sweet knowledge of my goodness and generated through the godly sorrow of the heart discovering its sinful nature. This self-awareness gives birth to a genuine contempt for one's sin and for the soul's selfish sensuality. It also creates a vibrant, sustaining humility. So you see, those who know genuine contrition and humility can suffer without growing impatient. In fact, that is how they repent.

—Catherine of Siena: *Dialogue*

MONDAY EVENING, FOURTH WEEK OF LENT

The Holy Spirit saw that it was hard to bring people to goodness because we have limited experience with godly sorrow and therefore possess only a shallow understanding of this purifying grief, so he designed the best pedagogy in the world—the Psalms. In these, the Holy Spirit combined the best teaching with the beauty of melody, understanding that while the music captured our attention, our hearts would soften to learn his wise instruction. A good doctor never gives a patient bad-tasting medicine without first putting in some honey.

For spiritual beginners, the Psalms are an alphabet. For those well on their journey, the Psalms are a way of improving what they know about God, while the very wise find the Psalms confirm everything they have learned about the Lord. The Psalms are the voice of the Church. They make any occasion joyful. They also create godly sorrow in us. The Psalms can elicit a tear from someone with a heart of stone. Psalms are the work of angels, a heavenly conversation, the wisdom of the greatest Teacher.

So, when we sing the Psalms, we are educating our souls in the best of ways. Through the Psalms, we learn practical lessons about Christlike behavior. Here, we find wounds are healed, weaknesses are made strong, strengths are turned to joy. We learn self-control and endurance. The Psalms soothe our souls and calm our minds. Singing Psalms binds friend to friend and stranger to stranger, for who can sing together to God and still hate his neighbor? In the Psalms we learn everything we need to know.

—Basil: *Commentary on Psalms*

TUESDAY MORNING, FOURTH WEEK OF LENT

Look at the silkworm. Only God could have planned the wonderful way silk is made. This fabric begins with an egg no bigger than a poppy seed. When the warm, sunny weather brings out the leaves on a mulberry tree, that tiny egg comes to life and grows into a silkworm caterpillar that constantly feeds on mulberry leaves until it becomes large enough to spin a silk cocoon around itself. Then this ugly white caterpillar buries itself in the cocoon, emerging utterly transformed—as a white butterfly.

The silkworm symbolizes the growing soul. Kindled by the Holy Spirit, the soul nourishes its life on the ordinary remedies God gives to us all, such as confession, religious books, sermons, Scripture, prayer, and contemplation. Using these, the soul begins spinning the house in which it must die. This house is Christ, as we read: Our "life is hidden with Christ in God." We are made to live in Christ, because he is our life. We must renounce self-love and self-will and pray, embracing godly sorrow as we remember the transient nature of things on earth, and then we must obey God by being kind to others.

Like the silkworm, we must be willing to envelope ourselves in Christ and then—through prayer— become dead to the things of this world. This process is how we become united with God. The transformation is so great that the soul does not recognize itself. As the silkworm changes in the cocoon from a repulsive, crawling grub into a white butterfly, so the soul transforms through godly sorrow, in Christ, from an ugly, sin-bound thing into a creature with wings of grace.

—Teresa of Avila: *Interior Castle*

TUESDAY EVENING, FOURTH WEEK OF LENT

Look at the wonderful friendship our kind Lord offers us! His tenderness protects us even while we sin. He gives us secret embraces, revealing our sins by the gentle light of his sweet mercy and grace. When we see ourselves as soul-dirty, we think then that God is angry with us and are encouraged by the Holy Spirit to feel godly sorrow and pray. We wish for nothing more than to change our immaturities and weaknesses and please God. We hope that God will forgive us, and of course he already has.

Then our caring Lord shows himself to the soul. God loves us, and so the Lord's countenance is the most cheerful one we will ever see. He welcomes the soul as a friend, embracing our souls as if they have experienced much pain and imprisonment, which they have. Our Lord is kind; he says, "Sweetheart, thank you for coming to me with your sorrow. Know this. I am always here with you. My love for you will turn your every grief into unceasing joy." That's how I came to understand that everything is made available to us through God's unending goodness.

—Julian of Norwich: *Revelations*

WEDNESDAY MORNING, FOURTH WEEK OF LENT

The song of rejoicing softens hard hearts. This song makes tears of godly sorrow flow within us. Singing summons the Holy Spirit. Praising and rejoicing offered in simplicity and love lead the faithful to complete harmony, where there's no discord.

So let those still living on earth sing and yearn for heavenly gold because divine grace banishes all dark obscurity. God's grace makes things that are usually dim to the bodily senses become pure and lucid. This inexhaustible, unmerited grace is why everyone who trusts God should offer the Lord loyal and tireless praises. Sing to God with joyful devotion, and never stop.

—Hildegard of Bingen: *Scivias*

WEDNESDAY EVENING, FOURTH WEEK OF LENT

Prayer is a gift. Whichever kind of prayer draws you to its practice, my teaching will help you know how best to engage in it for the good of your soul. For those of you who have lived deeply in the world, experiencing earthly human temptations firsthand, you may feel terrible regret when you convert to Christ, overcome by a good sadness. This is godly sorrow. As David prayed in the Psalms, you may find yourself crying out, "Have mercy on me, O God." To you, the Lord often gives the meditation on his humanity, on his nativity, or on his Passion, and when the Holy Spirit inspires this prayer in you, your soul will discover the most ineffable peace.

You will know you are being called to this prayer when your thoughts are suddenly pulled away from everything worldly, and in your soul you see the Lord as he was on earth, human. You will watch him seized like a thief, beaten, spat on, flogged, and condemned to death. You will see him carry the cross of our blackest guilt on his back. You will watch nails pierce his skin and fix him to the cross. You will see a crown of thorns clamped on his head and a sharp spear run through his body. Christ's passion will touch you deeply, stirring your compassion. Later, you may contemplate Christ's divine nature, but first you must practice meditating on his painful experience as a human.

This meditation will make Christ's passion personal to you. You will marvel that the Son of God has been this kind and patient and humble with someone as ungrateful and as imperfect as you. This realization will make you grieve intensely, and yet the paradox is that, in this grief, you will also experience the joy of tasting God's mercy. Accepting Christ's unending forgiveness will change your perspective, giving you an unspeakable joy for Christ's salvation through his Passion. This prayer is a kind of spiritual insight that brings you a genuine affection for and connection with God. It also helps you accept and conquer bad habits and develop virtues in your daily life.

St. Paul engaged in contemplative prayer and found it beneficial, saying, "I decided to know nothing among you except Jesus Christ, and him crucified." He also said, "May I never boast of anything except the cross of our Lord Jesus Christ, by which the world has been crucified to me, and I to the world."

—Walter Hilton: *Scale of Perfection*

Jesus is crucified

THE FORGIVING SACRIFICE

When they came to the place that is called The Skull, they crucified Jesus there with the criminals, one on his right and one on his left. Then Jesus said, "Father, forgive them; for they do not know what they are doing." And they cast lots to divide his clothing.
—Luke 23:33–34

It was nine o'clock in the morning when they crucified him. . . . In the same way the chief priests, along with the scribes, were also mocking him among themselves and saying, "He saved others; he cannot save himself."
—Mark 15:25, 31

[The prodigal son said,] "I will get up and go to my father, and I will say to him, 'Father, I have sinned against heaven and before you; I am no longer worthy to be called your son; treat me like one of your hired hands.'"
—Luke 15:18–19

At the tenth station, Jesus is crucified on the cross. As God, he can save himself, but he chooses not to. As a man unjustly accused and condemned, he hangs there between two criminals, and with nails in his body prays for the forgiveness of his murderers as they cast lots to divvy up his clothing and as the religious leaders of his day shout insults at him. This is the bloody truth of true forgiveness. It is sacrificial.

Forgiving always costs us something mortal and incontrovertible. We must suffer the death of our ego, the death of pride, the death of worry, the death of stupidity, the death of jealousy, the death of prejudice, the death of pettiness, the death of hatred, the death of laziness, the death of anger, and the death of self-absorption. Some even offer the sacrifice of the body, as does Christ, in physical death.

The collective, murderous anger of our world has never been more visible than on that hill at Calvary that shows where our every ugly word can lead, if given time. The mystic Hildegard of Bingen knows this truth—angry words are the seeds of cruel deeds—and in *Scivias* she tells us that her remedy is to meditate on the victory of Christ's cross: "When hatred tries to diminish who I am, I will look to the kindness of God's Son and to his pain. I will conquer my temper by accepting the thorns that release the delicate fragrance of roses, and bring honor to my Lord by learning to control my self."

It cost Jesus his life to redeem us from our deep-seated anger, as we find in the book of Isaiah:

> He was despised and rejected by others; a man of suffering and acquainted with infirmity; and as one from whom others hide their faces he was despised, and we held him of no account. Surely he has borne our infirmities and carried our diseases; yet we accounted him stricken, struck down by God, and afflicted. But he was wounded for our transgressions, crushed for our iniquities; upon him was the punishment that made us whole, and by his bruises we are healed.

And how are we so certain that if we had been at Golgotha, we would not have been holding the whip or hurling the insult? We must discover who we are and why we need forgiveness.

THURSDAY MORNING, FOURTH WEEK OF LENT

I will always remember that when the Creator spilled his blood, the world's four elements—earth, air, water, and fire—screamed, collapsed with grief, and shook from sadness.

Now, Father, with this bright red gift anoint our weaknesses.

—Hildegard of Bingen: *Scivias*

In the book Song of Solomon, we read, "Let me see your face." If we take this verse as our point of focus for meditating prayerfully on the Lord's passion, this spiritual exercise will refine our souls and purify our hearts.

So let us remember you, Lord, on the cross, where you were astonishingly bold. No one took your life from you, Creator. You offered it up. You suffered as a man, showing us your love, God. Your death gives us life, your selflessness gives us compassion, your sorrow informs our gladness, your exhaustion strengthens our enthusiasm, your difficulties comfort our souls, your loneliness is our companionship, and your giving of yourself is our forgiveness. We also remember that you grieved when Lazarus died. You wept. No one commanded you to resurrect your friend. You revived him because your love, kind Lord, is as strong as death.

—Bernard of Clairvaux: *Sermon*

THURSDAY EVENING, FOURTH WEEK OF LENT

The best object for contemplation is our Savior's cross. This tree is the center of eternity. When we look on the cross of Christ, we see the greatest miracle of all time—God's forgiveness. Looking on this cross, we enter into the heart of the universe. We see what angels most admire. We find the sweetest joy. The physical act of walking cannot take us there. No, we travel by soul. We must stop wandering the streets of this world, to meditate on the blood shed painfully on the cross. Fix your eyes on Christ there.

The Son of Man said, "When I am lifted up from the earth, [I] will draw all people to myself." What will draw us to him? Love. As children gather when a lion has been sighted, as people flock to a coronation, as a man is drawn to the one he loves, as a woman is drawn to the one she adores, as the sick are drawn to a physician, as the poor are pulled in by the generosity of a king, and as the hungry gather for a feast, so should we be drawn to the crucified Christ. They come voluntarily, and so should we.

The cross of Christ is the most immense, most valuable chest of treasures, the center of passion, the school of virtues, the house of wisdom, the throne of love, the theater of joy, the place of sorrow, the root of happiness, and the gate of heaven. It is the strangest thing on earth and in eternity, and the most important object of all time. When we look at Christ on the cross, we see a man loving the whole world. We see God dying for humanity. We see the rock of comfort, the fountain of joy, and the well of life filled with the blood of our Lord and Savior. The cross of Christ is the ladder by which we ascend into the highest heavens. Here we can learn patience, humility, self-denial, courage, discretion, enthusiasm, love, charity, contempt for the world, repentance, godly sorrow, modesty, loyalty, constancy, perseverance, holiness, forgiveness, and thanksgiving. If we contemplate the cross of Christ, we will learn how to imitate the love of Jesus.

—Thomas Traherne: *Centuries of Meditations*

FRIDAY MORNING, FOURTH WEEK OF LENT

In all that you do, remember that at the very end of time, you will stand before God the judge, from whom nothing is hidden. Nor does he accept bribes or excuses. Think how you fear an encounter with an angry earthly man, and now compare that fear with what you will feel as you come face-to-face with the God who knows your every sin. So plan ahead. Be preparing now to answer for yourself by doing the work of forgiveness.

People who are patient and godly grieve more over the malice of someone who injures them than they do for their own injury. Therefore, you must learn the good habit of praying for your enemies and forgiving those who offend you. You must never hesitate to ask others to forgive you your mistakes and offenses. You must also be someone who is more easily moved to compassion than to anger. Be willing to be hard on yourself in order to discipline your spirit.

It is better to make amends now for your sins and give up your vices than it is to keep them and have to answer for them on the Day of Judgment. The more we overlook our weaknesses now and indulge the flesh, the harder it will be later when we stand before the Lord and confess on the last day.

Ask for forgiveness and repent, so that Christ's peace will be yours now and at the end.

—Thomas à Kempis: *Imitation of Christ*

FRIDAY EVENING, FOURTH WEEK OF LENT

Some have said that since the heavenly Father knows what we need before we ask him, why should we pray? It is true that our Father and Creator loves us intimately and that he watches over us, whether or not we pray, just as a father protects his little children without waiting to be asked.

But let us consider this analogy carefully. What does it mean that we are God's children? Infants and toddlers are immature in articulating their demands—babies are too young to put their needs into words, while toddlers are old enough to express themselves but often clamor for the exact opposite of what they need. We ourselves behave even more childishly before God than children who rebel against their parents. It is absurd, but many people think they can pray and alter the mind of God who is unchanging and all-knowing.

Then why should we pray? We pray because this action changes us profoundly. How? Before you pray, you must first forgive anyone who has angered you for any reason, large or small, deserved or undeserved. Giving the gift of mercy is difficult for us; therefore, those who stand before God having forgiven people who wronged them have already received the best gift prayer can offer.

Prayer purifies us. We also benefit when we pray by picturing that God hears us and is standing beside us, listening to our supplications. This practice brings us closer to God. Praying every day also keeps us from sinning, and we can thereby accomplish much for God. Those who dedicate themselves to praying know this from experience. Prayer is our training in forgiveness.

To understand this truth, remember how you have been inspired by some wise person's example of morality and generosity. Reflecting on this person, you aspired to be like them, and this internal dialogue helped you discover that your worst impulses and uncontrollable emotions could be curbed and that you could learn new, better ways to handle difficult situations. How much more can our reflection on the Father of creation and salvation change us as we stand before our completely forgiving God and pray, knowing he is listening?

—Origen: *On Prayer*

SATURDAY MORNING, FOURTH WEEK OF LENT

Abba Moses wondered, "How can we make each day a new beginning?"

Abba Silvanus responded:

"Discover who you are. Be sorry for your sins. Do not feel superior to anyone, nor feel smug about others' weaknesses. Refuse to be a malicious gossip. Discipline yourself until your spirit is gentle. Forgive. Do not hate anybody, even if they hate you. Never return slander for slander. Refuse to become upset when others lie about you. Do not let yourself think badly of anyone, even in the privacy of your heart. This is the peace that passes understanding, and it can be yours if you refuse to judge others. Remember, Jesus commanded: 'Do not judge, so that you may not be judged.'"

And when someone asked Abba Silvanus, "How did you become so wise?" he answered, "I don't open my heart to angry thoughts."

A monk visited Abba Poemen to ask, "Do you ever have bad thoughts? If so, what do you do about them?"

Abba Poemen responded,

"Bad thoughts are like clothes stored in a trunk or closet. Over time, clothes turn yellow, get brown spots, and eventually fall apart. Leave them there, and they rot on their own. It's the same with your ungodly thoughts. Do not act on them, and they will disappear."

—*Sayings of the Fathers and Mothers*

SATURDAY EVENING, FOURTH WEEK OF LENT

If you are bickering, stop. End your quarrel as soon as you can. If you do not, your anger may escalate into hatred—the splinter becoming a beam. If you are not careful, over time, your heart can become the home of a murderer. The first letter of John says, "All who hate a brother or sister are murderers." If you have used words to attack someone verbally, go to that person right now and apologize.

If you are the victim in this situation, be quick to accept the apology. Forgive. You must never extend the argument at this point. Those who insult each other must forgive each other. If you do not, you are made into a liar whenever you pray the Lord's Prayer. Remember. If you are someone who prays often, your prayer must be especially genuine.

Do not be ashamed to use the same mouth that has offered cursing to now offer healing. Christ requires that we seek forgiveness. We must try to heal the wounds we cause. We should never let fear keep us from trying. Make this the work of your life: to live in harmony with others. Respect those with whom you live each day, remembering that we are all on the same path to God. Isn't everyone your neighbor? You must love them.

So be careful not to speak harshly to anyone, but if you do, quickly offer a healing word.

—Augustine: *Rule*

FIFTH SUNDAY MORNING OF LENT

Pride destroys many people, because they think they have accomplished something that no one else has ever done before. Then in their minds they start putting themselves ahead of others. If you let yourself feel superior to your brother or sister, you are ignorant about love. You cannot look down on your family and friends and still worship God. You must respect your neighbor, honor community, and obey the law of fellowship.

Many people leave Christ's path because they will not study how they can love the people they live with or work with or otherwise see on a daily basis. This respect is required of all who love Jesus. God has commanded that we love our neighbor. We must forgive each other, and we must encourage each other. We must also correct each other gently, not harshly, or we will make a brother or sister feel worse than they did before. If you must correct someone, remember your own faults as you do. Be as compassionate and as purposeful as a doctor setting a broken bone.

Nothing is better than love.

—Richard Rolle: *Fire of Love*

FIFTH SUNDAY EVENING OF LENT

On her last day on earth, the nun Macrina the Younger asked that her bed be turned eastward, toward the Resurrection. Then she whispered to Jesus:

"Eternal God, I was born in you. My soul has loved you with every ounce of strength I have received. I have respected you and your teachings, and I have worked at self-control, nailing my body to your cross, refusing to indulge every passing notion. Forgive me my sins because you can. Remember me, and welcome me home. Let a bright angel lead me there. Let your mercy rain down on me and wash me clean. Let me come before you, spotless, smelling like the sweetest incense.

"In your death on the cross, our fear of death met its death. When you volunteered to be both sin and law for us, you saved our lives from the fatal consequences of our rebellious hearts. This is forgiveness, your final sacrifice destroying the door to hell and fashioning the path of our resurrection. Your dying defeated death and put your cross in its place, to comfort us. Christ, you transformed our earthly existence into the beginning of true life. Your grace forever changed the ugly nature of mortality."

—Gregory of Nyssa: *Life of Macrina*

Jesus promises to share his reign with the good thief

THE JOY OF REDEMPTION

One of the criminals who were hanged there kept deriding him and saying, "Are you not the Messiah? Save yourself and us!" But the other rebuked him, saying, "Do you not fear God, since you are under the same sentence of condemnation? And we indeed have been condemned justly, for we are getting what we deserve for our deeds, but this man has done nothing wrong." Then he said, "Jesus, remember me when you come into your kingdom." He replied, "Truly I tell you, today you will be with me in Paradise."
—Luke 23:39–43

[The Lord says,] "I will give you as a light to the nations, that my salvation may reach to the end of the earth."
—Isaiah 49:6b

At the eleventh station, Jesus shows that his dying focus is not on himself but on loving any sinner who draws close to him. Even in the unlikeliest of places, on the torturous cross, Jesus honors the thief's simple confession of need and offers him, and us, redemption. Christ forgets his own suffering to listen to the concerns of this crook, teaching us to shift our attention away from our own complaints and pain toward sharing the Good News, the joy of our salvation, with anyone, anywhere.

In his conversation with the repentant thief, our Lord embodies his earlier teaching that all must come to him and rest there: "Come to me, all you that are weary and are carrying heavy burdens, and I will give you rest. Take my yoke upon you, and learn from me; for I am gentle and humble in heart, and you will find rest for your souls. For my yoke is easy, and my burden is light."

Sometimes we look on this humble thief and think how wonderful it is that Jesus in his last moments turns to offer him redemption, but too often we fail to see that we are that thief. For there are many ways to steal. We take back our promises, rob the truth of others' reputations as we slander them, and run away with a friend's joy when we argue—so we often break God's law. May we pray that when we sin we find ourselves close to Jesus in our abject suffering, for, as we see here, Christ is always listening and waiting for us to rely on him rather than on ourselves. He accepts the poverty of spirit that is this thief's most valuable possession offered up. And so Christ always accepts our poverty of spirit, too.

We are also the other, irascible thief, demanding, "Are you not the Messiah? Save yourself and us!" Whenever we encounter hardship, we ought not let ourselves grow impatient; instead, we should embrace this image of God hanging on the cross between a penitent lawbreaker and an angry one, and pray that we will always be the one turning to Christ in suffering and sin and asking him, "Remember me."

MONDAY MORNING, FIFTH WEEK OF LENT

Divine wisdom teaches us much about poverty. Poverty reveals our flaws because we see how destitute we are inside. This illumination makes God's goodness obvious to us, and we are able to accept his love without hesitation. Then we have the desire to share

God's love with others by being kind to them. Poverty of spirit can only exist when you have ceased relying on your own self. When you possess this truth, no devil can ever trick you.

That is why poverty is the mother of all virtues. She teaches divine wisdom. The wise Son of God knew poverty well. Daily, not just on the day he was crucified, the suffering God-man lived the poverty of the cross. Christ's life began, continued, and ended on the cross. Moment-by-moment, Jesus was on the cross of poverty, constant pain, scorn, and pure obedience. This is our heritage, and we must accept this cross as our birthright. Suffering lasts as long as we live, and the blessing is that we only receive the portion of it that we can bear. The more mature we become, the more we will love God and try to imitate the suffering God-man.

We see another example of true poverty in the good thief crucified beside the God-man. This thief lived a dishonest life, but once he accepted the divine light of God and saw God's goodness, he saw his own poverty immediately and embraced it. Then this thief asked the other criminal being crucified (the one insulting Christ): "You're being crucified, and yet you've no respect for God? We are getting what we deserve, but he has done nothing wrong. Can you not see that?" Then the penitent thief turned to Christ and said, "Remember me, Lord, when you enter your kingdom." He was saved then.

We sinners get no joy—no satisfaction—nor can we satisfy God until we confess our absolute poverty to him.

—Angela of Foligno: *Memorial; Instructions*

MONDAY EVENING, FIFTH WEEK OF LENT

What does it mean to be "made in God's image"? We read in Ephesians: "Be renewed in the spirit of your minds, and [. . .] clothe yourselves with the new self, created according to the likeness of God in true righteousness and holiness." At creation, the triune God emphasized the community necessary between God and his creatures, saying: "Let us make humankind in our image, according to our likeness." God's image shines in a person when an intimate dialogue exists between that person's soul, mind, emotions, will, and body and the Trinity.

The Trinity established its image in humanity so that we can possess in our very nature the ability to

126 - FOLLOWING CHRIST

live right. We must be kind, do good to those who need help, behave in a godly way, and make mature decisions. God wants the joy of intimacy with us, the kind a father has with his children. God is always delighted to see us. He loves all that he has made, and especially humanity, where his image is most clearly visible in our gifts of understanding, choosing, and remembering. The Trinity strengthens these traits in us.

An "image" is a reflection of something or someone else. God's image in us is God, but we are not God—instead, God is seen *through* us. An image cannot be seen in a mirror unless the mirror is shiny and clean, so as the soul grows, becoming purer, the image of God shines through us more clearly.

God's image in us is always teaching us love. Through it, we come to understand that we are made to practice unconditional kindness, live in joy, walk in peace, learn to rest, and nurture our health. Through God's image we learn to honor God. An image follows its pattern and is only genuine when both are in alignment. God's goodness in us shares everything good with us and requires that we, in turn, share all our good with others. Unhappiness comes when we break with God's image in us, dispossessing ourselves of our birthright. True happiness comes only when we allow the image of God in us every opportunity to unite us with our best desires. That is joy.

—Johann Arndt: *True Christianity*

TUESDAY MORNING, FIFTH WEEK OF LENT

Now I will tell you a story about a person who made a bad decision. Through this negative example, I can praise those of you who are staying true to Christ and so strengthen your joy in him.

There was a virgin in Alexandria who looked humble. Inside, however, she was arrogant. Although wealthy, she was stingy. She never gave even a small gift to a stranger in need, to a nun, or to a church. Nor did she listen to the Desert Fathers who told her that she must stop clinging to material possessions.

There was a priest named Abba Macarius in charge of a hospital for cripples. He decided to take matters into his own hands. So he came up with a scheme that might teach this woman how to love God. Everyone knew Macarius had been a lapidary in his youth, working with precious gems like sapphires and emeralds. One day, he approached this materialistic woman and made her an offer:

"Some jewels have come into my possession. They're at the house. I'm uncertain if they are treasure trove or stolen property, but I will sell them to you below their estimated value. Later, if you want, you can get your entire investment back by selling only one of these gems."

The woman greedily agreed without even thinking. Falling at Macarius's feet, she begged him, "Don't let anyone else have them!" Then she threw the money down right then and there, saying, "I do not want to see the man who's selling these." Macarius took her money and gave it immediately to support the hospital's needs.

Time went by, and the woman wondered where her gems were, but she was too hesitant to ask. Macarius had a reputation in Alexandria as someone who loved God and was generous and good. Even at the age of one hundred, he was a healthy and energetic servant of the Lord. Finally, though, the woman could wait no longer, so she met Macarius at the church. "Excuse me," she said, "but have you made a decision yet about those jewels?"

Macarius told her, "The minute I had your money, I deposited it. Please come with me to the hospital, and you can see the jewels."

At the hospital, women were housed on the second floor and men on the first. Macarius stood on the porch with her and asked, "Which do you want to see first, the sapphires or the emeralds?"

"You choose," she said. "I don't mind."

So Macarius took this wealthy virgin up to the second floor and showed her the women with crippled hands, twisted feet, and damaged faces, and he said, "Look! Here are your sapphires!"

Then Macarius the priest took her to see the men, also unable to walk, and he said, "See? Here are your emeralds. Do you like them? If not, I will return your money to you."

Turning from Macarius, she rushed out of the hospital and returned home. There she grieved so intensely she became ill, because she knew she had not been acting in a godly manner. Later, she went back to see the priest, and she thanked him.

—Palladius: *The Lausiac History*

TUESDAY EVENING, FIFTH WEEK OF LENT

When a person does something wrong and the soul realizes the mistake, the deed is like poison in the soul. On the other hand, a good deed is as sweet to the soul as good food is delicious to the body. The soul circulates through the body like sap through a tree, maturing a person the way sap enlivens a tree, turning it green and growing flowers and fruit.

Never let yourself forget that God's grace rewards not only those who never slip, but also those who bend and fall. So be joyful; sing and praise God always, because music stirs our hearts and engages our souls in ways we cannot describe. When this happens, we are taken beyond our earthly banishment back to the divine melody Adam knew when he sang with the angels and was whole in God, before his exile. The truth is that, before Adam refused God's fragrant flower of obedience, his voice was the best on earth. Why? Adam was made by the green thumb of God, who is the Holy Spirit. And if Adam had never lost the harmony God first offered him, and if we could hear the booming resonance of his original voice, the mortal fragilities each one of us possesses could not survive its strength.

—Hildegard of Bingen:
Scivias and *Letter to the Prelates of Mainz*

WEDNESDAY MORNING, FIFTH WEEK OF LENT

Jesus said, "Do not store up for yourselves treasures on earth, where moth and rust consume and where thieves break in and steal." These earthly "treasures" are anything that we obtain as credit for ourselves—maybe a shiny trophy or an award. In God's eyes, this desire for recognition buries whatever good we do deep in the earth, where it rusts in its own vanity or sees the moths of pride eating holes into it. Either way, good deeds done to gain attention contribute nothing of value to the soul. That is why we must constantly be on the lookout for pride, daily searching the innermost rooms of our hearts for vanity. We must carefully trace the footsteps that come in and out of our souls; otherwise, some beast—a lion or dragon—might slip in and make his home there, followed by snakes and other creatures. We must learn in every moment to turn to God's good news, not forgetting its power to bring us joy.

Every day, grab the gospel plow, which is the constant reflection on our Lord's Cross. Don't let go. Use this divine tool to break up, turn over, and soften the ground of your heart. It is the only way we can rid ourselves of the deadly beasts lurking in our hearts' most hidden lairs.

—John Cassian: *Conferences*

WEDNESDAY EVENING, FIFTH WEEK OF LENT

Abba Moses' humility was well-known among the Desert Fathers. He had become a monk late in life. Before that, he had been a slave, then a gang member and a robber. These experiences informed his teaching. Abba Moses often said to his community, "God doesn't listen to your prayers unless you are certain you're a sinner."

One brother asked, "What do you mean?"

Abba Moses said, "If you know your shortcomings, you know you're not perfect. If you see your own mistakes, you don't have eyes for your neighbor's sins."

—*Sayings of the Fathers and Mothers*

The joy of divine companionship is possible when you humbly participate in the redemption of Christ. So be as conscientious in your work as the bee in the honeycomb, or all will be lost. Do not forget, however, that the bee does leave its hive from time to time in search of flowers, so, too, should the soul cease from thinking of itself sometimes to meditate on the glory and majesty of God. Turn the eyes of your soul on Christ now, and rejoice in his beautiful image.

—Teresa of Avila: *Way of Perfection* and *Interior Castle*

Jesus is on the cross,
with his mother and disciple below

THE COMMUNITY OF AGAPE LOVE

Meanwhile, standing near the cross of Jesus were his mother, and his mother's sister, Mary the wife of Clopas, and Mary Magdalene. When Jesus saw his mother and the disciple whom he loved standing beside her, he said to his mother, "Woman, here is your son." Then he said to the disciple, "Here is your mother." And from that hour the disciple took her into his own home.

—John 19:25–27

If I speak in the tongues of mortals and of angels, but do not have love, I am a noisy gong or a clanging cymbal. And if I have prophetic powers, and understand all mysteries and all knowledge, and if I have all faith, so as to remove mountains, but do not have love, I am nothing. If I give away all my possessions, and if I hand over my body so that I may boast, but do not have love, I gain nothing. Love is patient; love is kind; love is not envious or boastful or arrogant or rude. It does not insist on its own way; it is not irritable or resentful; it does not rejoice in wrongdoing, but rejoices in the truth. It bears all things, believes all things, hopes all things, endures all things. Love never ends.

—1 Corinthians 13:1–8a

At the twelfth station, Jesus takes care of his mother in her grief; he also looks after his disciple John. By entrusting them to each other, he shows us how important community is and how responsible we are for taking care of each other. Christ's selflessness is both a comfort and a challenge. We see that as his suffering approaches the climax of death, he thinks only of his family and friend. This image of Jesus, Mary, and John is a tableau of true agape love. First, Mary and John suffer with Jesus to the ignominious end of the Cross, while Jesus is concerned for their futures on earth and so reminds them both that they will need each other.

May this scene teach us the truth of the opening words of the Lord's Prayer, "Our Father." It is easy to forget that we are all related in Christ. As we read in 1 Timothy, we are to love each other as family: "Do not speak harshly to an older man, but speak to him as to a father, to younger men as brothers, to older women as mothers, to younger women as sisters—with absolute purity."

THURSDAY MORNING, FIFTH WEEK OF LENT

What did Mary, the mother of our Lord, wrap baby Jesus in? Taking a coarse gray blanket out from under Joseph's saddle on the donkey's back, she wrapped the hardy Savior in this blanket and placed her son gently in the crib. Immediately, Jesus began crying like a newborn baby does. As long as babies are unable to speak, they never cry except to express a real need. Baby Jesus, our Lord, wept—despite his noble nature— because he was put to bed in a cowshed, for our base sin. Christ wept for all the world, hiding his happiness. Jesus wept for all the world, hiding his power.

Mary speaks, "When I stood under the cross feeling lonesome and dead, the sword of Jesus' physical suffering cut me deeply, wounding my soul. But first, when I was young, I nursed baby Jesus."

—Mechthild of Magdeburg:
The Flowing Light of the Godhead

THURSDAY EVENING, FIFTH WEEK OF LENT

Our labor here is brief, our reward eternal. Remember this. Do not let the pleasures of this world—which vanish like dew—excite you. Refuse the fake delights of this deceptive world. Never let them trick you. Close your ears to hell's whispers. Be brave and resist them. Smile and endure when things go wrong, and never let success go to your head.

Instead, look to Christ who goes before us. Take up the cross, and follow him. Do not let the thought of Jesus leave your mind. Meditate constantly on the mysteries of the Cross and the pain his mother must have felt standing there below him.

Pray. Always be alert.

—Clare of Assisi: *Letters*

FRIDAY MORNING, FIFTH WEEK OF LENT

Grateful for the Unobtrusive Good

Mary, whatever's small and unnoticed
is like you . . . growing,
the greenest twig
stirring
in the rainy gusts that were all those questions
asked by those who lived before your time and
spent their lives looking for God's Son to come.
The sunshine warmed you,
and when the time was ripe,
you blossomed,
smelling like balsam,
and the fragrance of your Bloom
renewed the spices' dry perfume.
The earth rejoiced when your body grew
wheat. The sky celebrated by giving
the grass dew, and the birds built
nests in your wheat, and the food
of the Eucharist was made for all humanity.
We feast on it, full of joy.

—Hildegard of Bingen: *Hymn*

FRIDAY EVENING, FIFTH WEEK OF LENT

One day I felt exhausted because I had worn myself out. I asked the Lord, "What is wrong with me? What should I do?"

The Lord answered me, "I'll comfort you just like a mother comforts her child. Have you never watched a mother embracing her child?"

I went silent. I could not remember, so the Lord reminded me of the time six months earlier that I had watched a mother bending down and holding her little child close to her. He pointed out some things I had not noticed at the time. The mother often asked her toddler to kiss her, and to do this, the child had to work hard to raise himself up on little legs to reach her cheek. The Lord recommended that I, too, work hard and raise myself up through contemplation back to enjoying his sweet love.

God also pointed out that when this toddler spoke, nobody else there could understand what the little child was saying, except the mother. In this same way, only God can understand what a person wants and intends to do, and only God judges a person appropriately, while other people only see exteriors

—Gertrude the Great: *The Herald of Divine Love*

SATURDAY MORNING, FIFTH WEEK OF LENT

Mother is such a beautiful word, so full of sweetness and all that is good, that it really can only be used to describe Jesus. Motherhood is the agape love existing between a woman and the baby at her breast. It is wise, good, and smart, and even though our corporeal birth is small and simple when compared to our invisible spiritual birth and life, we must remember that Jesus is in the middle of even our corporeal birth—and that without his divine touch, we would not have been born to two earthly parents.

Kind earthly mothers are intimately aware of and responsive to their child's every need. A mother protects and nurtures her child. That is what a mother does. A child will change as he or she grows up, and to accommodate that change and growing independence, a good mother will alter her approach to her child, but not her love.

Mothers also scold their children when their children act on some of their less-appropriate desires, because all loving mothers want to root out bad decisions and unhealthy habits and plant good character in their children. Our Lord is kind to us in this same way.

Our Lord is our mother, who wants us to be secure in God. We help God parent us when we love him, and this love we have for God is set in motion by the generosity of the God-man born a baby; for Christ is always telling us, "Remember you love me. Remember who you are, and whose."

Mothers give their children milk, but Jesus is the sweet mother who feeds us with himself. His kindness accomplishes this nourishment when we eat the holy Eucharist. This priceless food is life itself, strengthening us and helping us grow. So Jesus says, "The holy church teaches you about me." This statement means that Jesus animates the Eucharist and through it heals us and helps us live abundant lives by being kind to each other.

Mothers also lay their children down on their breasts, for rest and succor, but Jesus is the gentlest mother who takes us by the hand and leads us into God's breast through his own satisfying open side. I saw Jesus look down there at his gashed side and smile and say to me, "Look here and see how I love you."

So, when we sin and remorseful feelings hit, God wants us to remember we are his children. Hurt, upset, or frightened children always run directly to their mother and fling their arms around her. Then they hug their mother with all their might. God wants us to do just that. We must act like the trusting, much-loved children that we are.

God loves us completely and wants our love, and if we trust him, all will be well.

—Julian of Norwich: *Revelations*

SATURDAY EVENING, FIFTH WEEK OF LENT

The least of God's poor children, I give thanks to the Lord because from the day I started living by the monastic rule until today, God's hand has been on me, and I have constantly experienced his arrows in my body. My many long illnesses have affected not only me, but also the sisters with whom I live in community. May the Lord bless them for their motherly affection toward me in my suffering.

Whenever I was so sick I could control no part of my body except my tongue, I still—and I say this without arrogance—meditated tenaciously on the Psalms. Then, when paralysis stopped even my tongue, my mind satisfied its duty.

It would bore you if I told you of the hardships I have endured because of my illnesses. You know the material possessions of our house are modest. But the Father of orphans, our Lord, is worried about me, and through his grace all my grief turns to joy in my heart. In all things, may God—the Comforter of the humble—be magnified.

—Elisabeth of Schönau, *First Book of Visions*

PALM, OR PASSION, SUNDAY MORNING

In the conversation that is community, whatever is twisted in us will be straightened and whatever is good will be strengthened. The humble sharing that creates community helps us avoid being condemned with those who are only wise in their own eyes.

—Basil: *Rule*

The Word who made the world also remade it. Creation and salvation originate in the same love. Through the incarnation of Jesus, God saved the world through the one who first made the world. When our omnipotent Father created us humans through his Word, God wanted us to have a meaningful relationship with him, so he made us in his own image, for us to make community.

But, in spite of the wonderful nature of God's love, we often refuse his gifts, choosing selfish, divisive pleasures of the moment instead. What was God supposed to do? He had no choice but to renew his image in humanity, so we could come to know him again. The only way he could do this was to send the image of himself, our Savior Jesus Christ, as his messenger. So God's Word became a person. He assumed a human body to destroy death once and for all and restore God's image in us.

It is very similar to what happens when an oil portrait is damaged by water and the image is ruined. In spite of the defect, the painter does not throw away the canvas. The subject of the portrait is asked to come back and sit for it again. Then the artist redraws the work on the same canvas. That is what happened when the Son of God, who is the image of our Father, came and lived with us, to restore humanity and reestablish community. He came looking for his lost sheep, as he says in the Gospel of Luke: "[I] came to seek out and to save the lost."

—Athanasius of Alexandria: *On the Incarnation*

PALM, OR PASSION, SUNDAY EVENING

I am the least, the weakest, the most common person on earth, Lord, and I beg you, my heavenly Father, Christ, Spirit, holy Trinity, to forgive me today of all my sins of omission, committed in your holy service. Forgive not only those sins I committed while seeking to improve my life or out of necessity, but also those that I committed because of sinful spite, which I could have easily stopped if I had just felt like it.

Please accept, Lord, this tiny improvement in my will, and help me change what in me is spiritually stupid because I want to lead a holy life and have community with your saints on earth.

—Mechthild of Magdeburg:
The Flowing Light of the Godhead

Jesus dies on the cross

THE TRUST OF LISTENING

It was now about noon, and darkness came over the whole land until three in the afternoon, while the sun's light failed; and the curtain of the temple was torn in two. Then Jesus, crying with a loud voice, said, "Father, into your hands I commend my spirit." Having said this, he breathed his last.
—Luke 23:44–46

At three o'clock Jesus cried out with a loud voice, "Eloi, Eloi, lema sabachthani?" which means, "My God, my God, why have you forsaken me?"
—Mark 15:34

Hear the voice of my supplication, as I cry to you for help, as I lift up my hands toward your most holy sanctuary.
—Psalm 28:2

At the thirteenth station, Jesus dies on the cross. The mystery is that Christ's trust in God leads him here, to death of the most agonizing sort, after a miscarriage of justice; but he shows us that, though he feels utterly forsaken as he redeems the world's sins, Christ is still listening for God at the very end, crying out, "My God, my God, why have you forsaken me?"

We remember that Job in his terrible suffering cursed the day of his birth: "Let the stars of its dawn be dark; let it hope for light, but have none; may it not see the eyelids of the morning—because it did not shut the doors of my mother's womb, and hide trouble from my eyes. 'Why did I not die at birth, come forth from the womb and expire?'"

Both examples give us reason to remain in dialogue with our Creator. Since God's ways are not our ways, we do well to remember God's questioning of Job, after Job's repeated complaints:

> Where were you when I laid the foundation of the earth? Tell me, if you have understanding. Who determined its measurements—surely you know! Or who stretched the line upon it? On what were its bases sunk, or who laid its cornerstone when the morning stars sang together and all the heavenly beings shouted for joy? Or who

shut in the sea with doors when it burst out
from the womb?—when I made the clouds its
garment, and thick darkness its swaddling band,
and prescribed bounds for it, and set bars and
doors, and said, "Thus far shall you come, and
no farther, and here shall your proud waves be
stopped"? Have you commanded the morning
since your days began, and caused the dawn
to know its place? . . . Is it by your wisdom that
the hawk soars, and spreads its wings toward
the south? Is it at your command that the eagle
mounts up and makes its nest on high? . . . Shall
a faultfinder contend with the Almighty? Anyone
who argues with God must respond.

Job's response to God's questioning is the beginning
of wisdom: "I have uttered what I did not understand,
things too wonderful for me, which I did not know.
Hear, and I will speak."

MONDAY MORNING OF HOLY WEEK

Listen! I want to tell you the best dream I ever had!
  At midnight,
when everything was absolutely quiet, and all creatures
who could speak were fast asleep, I thought I saw
the most amazing tree soaring through the sky,
the brightest beacon I'd ever seen, wound
with light, covered in gold and jewels.
Beautiful angels flocked to it, staring.
I thought to myself, *This can't be a cross of shame,*
because every eye in the world fixed on it.
And in that moment, I knew two things, that
this was the wonderful tree of victory and
that I was sin-stained and shame-wounded.
The tree of glory glowed, but through its
    golden clothes
I saw blood seeping out from the ancient struggle
    for a lost humanity.
Bleeding on its right side,
it completely overwhelmed me with sorrow.
This vision's truth and beauty scared me.
Then I saw the living beacon changing,
from being wet with sweat, then drenched
    with blood,

then crusted with treasure, and I lay there a long
    time, grieving,
looking at the Savior's tree, until it broke
    the silence,
calling out to me, and this most excellent tree said:

> It was years ago. I still remember being cut
> down at the edge of the forest. They slashed
> me down. Powerful enemies seized me for
> their executions. They forced me to crucify their
> criminals. Soldiers carried me on their shoulders
> to that hill and set me up there. And then I saw a
> wonder. The Lord of all humanity running bravely
> toward me as if he wished to climb up, and I
> couldn't bow, couldn't break, couldn't disobey
> his Word, even as the earth shook all around me.
> Yes, I could have destroyed the enemy, but I stood
> fast watching the young hero, who is almighty
> God. His body as strong as his will, he stripped
> himself and mounted the gallows of the cross, and
> ransomed all humanity. Many saw his courage.
>
> I trembled when this Warrior embraced me.
> But I dared not bend, dared not fall. Raised up
> as a rood, I held a hero, our King, the ruler of
> heaven. I had to obey the Lord. I had to stay

fast as they drove dark nails in me, their awful blows leaving deep, obvious scars, but I could not harm a soul. They smeared us both with their lies, and I was drenched in the blood gushing from that man's side.

On that hill I saw the Creator crucified. Is there a worse fate? Clouds of darkness covered the bright light of the King's body. Shadows swept the earth. All creation wept. Christ was on the cross. I saw it all, wounded with sorrow and brought low, but I bent to the hands of those men, obedient. God's Son suffered on me a while. And that is why I am glorious and powerful and raised on high today, healing all who bow to me.

—Anonymous Old English Poet:
The Dream of the Rood

MONDAY EVENING OF HOLY WEEK

Can anyone say, "I have no weaknesses"? Can anyone say they have never been depressed? Who has never felt as lonesome as a homeless beggar? Life can be overwhelming at times. You can become exhausted and in need of encouragement. When you do, turn to Psalm 102. Imagine that its words are your own. Say them to yourself, and they will become yours. Rest in God and trust him; meditate on these words, and your soul will learn how to deal with emotions in a godly way. Let us listen to these verses together:

> Hear my prayer, O LORD; let my cry come to you. Do not hide your face from me in the day of my distress. Incline your ear to me; answer me speedily on the day when I call. For my days pass away like smoke, and my bones burn like a furnace. My heart is stricken and withered like grass; I am too wasted to eat my bread. Because of my loud groaning my bones cling to my skin. I am like an owl of the wilderness, like a little owl of the waste places. I lie awake; I am like a lonely bird on the housetop. All day long my enemies taunt me; those who deride me use my name for a curse. For I eat ashes like bread, and mingle tears with my drink, because of your indignation and anger; for you have lifted me up and thrown me aside. My days are like an evening shadow; I wither away like grass. But you, O LORD, are

enthroned forever; your name endures to all generations. You will rise up and have compassion on Zion, for it is time to favor it; the appointed time has come. For your servants hold its stones dear, and have pity on its dust. The nations will fear the name of the LORD, and all the kings of the earth your glory. For the LORD will build up Zion; he will appear in his glory. He will regard the prayer of the destitute, and will not despise their prayer. Let this be recorded for a generation to come, so that a people yet unborn may praise the LORD: that he looked down from his holy height, from heaven the LORD looked at the earth, to hear the groans of the prisoners, to set free those who were doomed to die; so that the name of the LORD may be declared in Zion, and his praise in Jerusalem, when peoples gather together, and kingdoms, to worship the LORD. He has broken my strength in midcourse; he has shortened my days. "O my God," I say, "do not take me away at the midpoint of my life, you whose years endure throughout all generations." Long ago you laid the foundation of the earth, and the heavens are the work of your hands. They

will perish, but you endure; they will all wear out
like a garment. You change them like clothing,
and they pass away; but you are the same, and
your years have no end. The children of your
servants shall live secure; their offspring shall
be established in your presence.

—Athanasius of Alexandria: *A Letter to Marcellinus*

TUESDAY MORNING OF HOLY WEEK

We worship God, whose reason ordered, whose Word
commanded, and whose power made this universe
from nothing. The Creator is invisible, but the
Father may be seen: "The heavens are telling the
glory of God, and the firmament proclaims his
handiwork. . . . Their voice goes out through all
the earth, and their words to the end of the world."
God cannot physically be touched, but his grace
makes him ever present to us in his Word, who is
called the *Logos*. The Father designed creation, the
Logos set our world in motion, and his Spirit per-
vades the universe.

This Spirit is called the Son of God and also the
divine God, since in essence they are one because

God is also Spirit. An example may help illuminate this mystery. A ray leaves the sun, radiating outward, but it is still a part of the whole because the sun itself is in that ray. The fundamental nature of the sun is not divided but extended. In the same way, the Spirit emanates from Spirit—God from God, and Light from Light. That is why the one who was born of God is both God and the Son of God. Prophets preached that this ray of God would be the child of a virgin and take on the flesh of humanity and be both God and man, and that divinity would nourish his body. And he grew up, spoke, taught, worked, and is Christ.

Today, the church is the Spirit of God in whom the Trinity of the one divinity—Father, Son, and Holy Spirit—lives.

And yet the principal crime of the human race, the highest guilt charged against us, is that we often trust the world, with all its illogicality, more than we trust the *Logos*.

—Tertullian: *Apology* and *On Idolatry*

TUESDAY EVENING OF HOLY WEEK

Here is what a friendship with our dearest companion, our holiest God, is like. In it, intimacy is always possible, and this closeness cannot be stopped, except on our side, for God is always open to us. Nothing can come between us and God, and we can be alone with God whenever we want, for as long as we want. All we have to do is desire it.

So close the door on your worldly plans and conversations and deadlines and live instead in paradise with the God of love. If we desire this closeness that comes from shutting the door on the world, we must realize that that door is our hearts. You do not have to be a mystic to accomplish this communion. You only need to focus on God with your will. That is all you must do. God loves you and is waiting for your intention.

Do not confuse this state with empty silence. I am speaking of a turning inward and a listening.

—Teresa of Avila: *The Way of Perfection*

Little by little, God grows us ever more in grace because God wants to be seen and sought. God wants to be awaited and trusted.

—Julian of Norwich: *Revelations*

WEDNESDAY MORNING OF HOLY WEEK

Teachers must always adapt their approach to their audience. Of course, every teacher has points to make and principles to share, but—more than any abstract knowledge—a teacher must know the actual individuals sitting there and listening. What are their needs? How can they be reached? Where are they in their journey with God?

It is helpful to think of the minds of those listening in the audience as if they were the taut, well-tuned strings of a beautiful harp. A sensitive, talented harpist will play these in different ways to create the harmony of music. If the musician used only one kind of stroke, only cacophonous sounds would result.

In the same way, anyone who ministers to others must remember that no two people are alike. Any audience is diverse—the young and the old, the rich and the poor, naturally happy people and those who are depressed, dedicated worker bees and diligent administrators, slaves and masters, the wise and the careless, the outgoing and the shy, the impatient and the unflustered, the kindhearted and the jealous, the genuine and the fake, the healthy and the sick, those who live cautiously because they always fear getting into trouble and those whose hearts are so hard that they never fear anything, the introverted and the talker, the conscientious and the lazy, the slow-to-speak and the angry, the humble and the arrogant, the trustworthy and the unreliable, the glutton and the one who fasts, the generous givers and those who steal. The list is unending.

—St. Gregory the Great: *Pastoral Care*

WEDNESDAY EVENING OF HOLY WEEK

Choose Christ as your life model. Follow the suffering God-man. Learn from his life. Listen to his teachings. Take all your desire and chase God down with it. Work to reach his Cross.

See how Christ gave himself as an example? Jesus told us to look at him with the eyes of our souls. God said: "Learn from me because I am gentle, and my soul is humble. And you will find rest for your hearts here."

Pay attention to what Christ did not say. He did not say, "Learn to fast from me" or "Learn to scorn the world and live in poverty" or "Learn from me how to perform great miracles," although he did each of these things well. No, instead Jesus said, "Learn from me because I'm gentle and humble in my soul."

The point is that Christ made humility and gentleness the foundation for every other virtue. Nothing else matters. Not integrity, not fasting, not poverty, not shabby clothing, not years of good works, not the accomplishment of miracles—none of these is important without a humble, listening heart.

—Angela of Foligno: *Instructions*

MAUNDY THURSDAY MORNING

Lord, you are my Mother, and more than my Mother. My earthly mother was in labor a day or a night delivering me, but you, my beautiful, sweet Savior, were in labor for me over thirty years. How you labored in love for me your whole life. But when it came time for you to deliver me, your labor pains were so terrible that your sacred sweat fell on the earth in huge drops of blood. When the hour came for you to give birth to me, you were placed on the hard bed of the cross— your nerves and all your veins ruptured.

Surely it is no surprise your veins burst when in a single day you gave birth to the whole world.

—Marguerite d'Oingt: *Page of Meditations*

MAUNDY THURSDAY EVENING

The soul's courage never weakens, and its will never hesitates in seeking, asking, learning, gaining, and retaining everything that can help bring it to Love. All the soul's searching, teaching, praying to God, and meditating are for this one purpose—to get into the presence of God and become Love, and to live a moral life with the purity that is the signature of true love. Such a soul always considers what it is and what it ought to be, what it possesses and what it lacks. With its whole attention, and with great yearning and all its strength, the soul tries to keep itself pure and to shun everything that could burden it and slow it down as it works to accomplish spiritual growth.

The soul must live in hope.

—Beatrijs of Nazareth, *Seven Manners of Living*

If you want to grow the faith of your soul, read Scripture with humility and simplicity, never making it your goal to gain a reputation for being "learned." Read the wise words of ancient Christians also, and let them work their purpose in you. For the wiser a person is and the simpler the heart, the more Christ's light can enter into a person's life, and that which seems naturally impossible to us becomes possible through Christ's grace. So do not be discouraged when a problem arises. Consider painful circumstances helpful. They're good for your soul. Instead, let Christ strengthen you with his heavenly courage.

　　　　　—Thomas à Kempis: *Imitation of Christ*

My whole life, I was looking for this:

> Let the same mind be in you that was in Christ Jesus, who, though he was in the form of God, did not regard equality with God as something to be exploited, but emptied himself, taking the form of a slave, being born in human likeness. And being found in human form, he humbled himself and became obedient to the point of death—even death on a cross.

I was looking for Christ-centered knowledge, but I was blind, not knowing I needed Christ's humility, hidden from the wise and intelligent, and revealed to infants. I finally found it when you, Christ, helped me go inside my inner self and look with the eye of my soul and see your light—which is nothing like the light we see with our bodies—for your light is pure love. How did I ever doubt? Why did I ever struggle?

I might as well have asked, "Am I alive?" as to wonder if you love me.

Only Jesus is the foundation of our humility.

—Augustine: *Confessions*

GOOD FRIDAY MORNING

Death, be not proud, though some have called you
Mighty and dreadful, for you are not so;
For those, whom you think you do overthrow,
Die not, poor Death, nor yet can you kill me.
From rest and sleep, which but your pictures be,
Much pleasure, then from you much more must flow,
And soonest our best men with you do go,
Rest of their bones, and soul's delivery.
You're slave to Fate, chance, kings, and desperate men,
And do with poison, war, and sickness dwell,
And poppy, or charms can make us sleep as well,
And better than your stroke; why swell you then?
One short sleep past, we wake eternally,
And Death shall be no more; Death, you shall die.

—John Donne: *Holy Sonnet X*

Jesus is placed in the tomb

THE BIRTH OF COURAGE

When it was evening, there came a rich man from Arimathea, named Joseph, who was also a disciple of Jesus. He went to Pilate and asked for the body of Jesus; then Pilate ordered it to be given to him. So Joseph took the body and wrapped it in a clean linen cloth and laid it in his own new tomb, which he had hewn in the rock. He then rolled a great stone to the door of the tomb and went away.

—Matthew 27:57–60

Set me as a seal upon your heart, as a seal upon your arm; for love is strong as death, passion fierce as the grave. Its flashes are flashes of fire, a raging flame.

—Song of Solomon 8:6

Wait for the Lord; be strong, and let your heart take courage; wait for the Lord!

—Psalm 27:14

At the fourteenth station, Christ is in the tomb, his body cold. And Peter, James, and John, and all who have chosen to follow him find their grief is mingled with the rawest fear imaginable. Having left their old lives to follow Jesus, they now find their leader gone. They are bewildered, not realizing yet that Christ will rise again. To them, this is the end, not a beginning.

We must learn from the disciples' doubt. What we perceive as death is often the stillness before the eruption of new life. We must realize that waiting on God is always fruitful. It teaches us not to be fearful. Christ's bitter experience in the tomb thaws our hearts and gives us the courage to love.

GOOD FRIDAY EVENING

Christ's crucifixion cross told this story: Then the disciples came and got almighty God and took him down. These warriors left me standing there, all covered in blood. I was injured, battle-scarred. They put him, deadly tired, down, then stood at the head of his body, looking at heaven's Lord, as he rested there a spell, unmoving, fully exhausted after his crucial fight. His warriors began digging a grave for him in full view of me, his murderer. They carved it out of bright stone and put the Lord of victories in it. Then they sang a song of grief. They were miserable and worn out, too, and when they left their excellent Prince and went home, he rested there, alone.

But we crosses stood there a long time after the warriors had gone, and we wept as his corpse, that beautiful temple of life, grew cold. Then men began to chop us down. It was an awful way to end a terrible day. Someone buried us in a deep pit, but the Lord's followers—his friends—heard I was there, so they came for me, to decorate me in gold and silver.

Now you've heard my confession, how I endured these crimes, pain, agony, and loss, so it's time for people all over the world to worship me and pray to his cross. Once the harshest, most hated punishment, I revealed the way of Life and Truth, because the Prince of glory and Lord of heaven honored me above all other trees. I command you, my much-loved companion—tell others. Publish these words: *On the tree of glory almighty God suffered for humanity's many sins and Adam's ancient mistake. The Lord tasted death there, but then he rose up, ready to help us with his mighty courage.*

—Anonymous Old English Poet:
The Dream of the Rood

HOLY SATURDAY MORNING

Set your heart on God. Make your love and your will one act. God is not silence, nor speaking; not fasting, nor eating; not loneliness, nor friendship. God is in neither of the two sides of any paradox. Instead, God is hidden between these, and nothing your mind does can help you find him—not your reason, not your thoughts, not studying—only your love. God can be loved, yes.

The genuinely loving heart can choose to find God. Love, and the sharp arrow of your simple longing will not fail to reach its mark, who is God. Contemplate God, rest in not seeing and not knowing, and you will experience the dark mystery of everything beyond our understanding. Then—and only then—does God sometimes flash out a spiritual ray of light for you, piercing the cloud of unknowing between you and him, and allowing you a glimpse of his secrets, which are beyond anybody's ability to describe.

—Anonymous: *Discretion of Stirrings*
and the *Cloud of Unknowing*

HOLY SATURDAY EVENING

The Holy Spirit animates   all,
moves   all,
     roots   all,
       forgives   all,
         cleanses   all,
           erases   all
our past mistakes and then
puts medicine on our wounds.
We praise God's Spirit of incandescence
for awakening and reawakening
all creation.

Spirit of fire, Paraclete, our Comforter, you are the *Live* in *alive*, the *Be* in every creature's *being*, the *Breathe* in every breath on earth. Holy Life-Giver, Doctor of the desperate, Healer of everyone broken past hope, Medicine for all wounds, Fire of love, Joy of hearts, fragrant Strength, sparkling Fountain, Protector, Penetrator, in you we contemplate how God goes looking for those who are lost and reconciles those who are at odds with him.

Break our chains!

You bring people together. You curl clouds, whirl winds, send rain on rocks, sing in creeks, and turn the lush earth green.

You teach those who listen, breathe joy and
wisdom into them.

We praise you for these gifts,

Light-giver, Sound of joy, Wonder of being alive,
Hope of every person,

you are our strongest Good.

—Hildegard of Bingen: *Hymns*

Jesus rises from the dead

THE PREPARATION ON EARTH FOR ETERNAL LIFE

Early on the first day of the week, while it was still dark, Mary Magdalene came to the tomb and saw that the stone had been removed from the tomb. So she ran and went to Simon Peter and the other disciple, the one whom Jesus loved, and said to them, "They have taken the Lord out of the tomb, and we do not know where they have laid him." Then Peter and the other disciple set out and went toward the tomb. The two were running together, but the other disciple outran Peter and reached the tomb first. He bent down to look in and saw the linen wrappings lying there, but he did not go in. Then Simon Peter came, following him, and went into the tomb. He saw the linen wrappings lying there, and the cloth that had been on Jesus' head, not lying with the linen wrappings but rolled up in a place by itself. Then the other disciple, who reached the tomb first, also went in, and he saw and believed; for as yet they did not understand the scripture, that he must rise from the dead. Then the disciples returned to their homes.

But Mary stood weeping outside the tomb. As she wept, she bent over to look into the tomb; and she saw two angels in white, sitting where the body of Jesus had been lying, one at the head and the other at the feet. They said to her, "Woman, why are you weeping?" She said to them, "They have taken away my Lord, and I do not know where they have laid him." When she had said this, she turned around and saw Jesus standing there, but she did not know that it was Jesus. Jesus said to her, "Woman, why are you weeping? Whom are you looking for?" Supposing him to be the gardener, she said to him, "Sir, if you have carried him away, tell me where you have laid him, and I will take him away." Jesus said to her, "Mary!" She turned and said to him in Hebrew, "Rabbouni!" (which means Teacher). Jesus said to her, "Do not hold on to me, because I have not yet ascended to the Father. But go to my brothers and say to them, 'I am ascending to my Father and your Father, to my God and your God.'" Mary Magdalene

went and announced to the disciples, "I have seen the Lord"; and she told them that he had said these things to her.
—John 20:1–18

My heart is steadfast, O God, my heart is steadfast. I will sing and make melody.
—Psalm 57:7

At the fifteenth station, Jesus rises from the dead. In all of the shouting and triumph on Easter morning, we do well to remember that, as we have seen throughout this devotional, it is just as awesome, and in some ways maybe even more so, that God has become human. God is born, is loved, loves, makes friends, works, eats, is worried and betrayed, is wrongly accused, suffers horribly, and dies. How wonderful that Christ rises from the dead, and how equally wonderful it is that God has become human, and our constant friend. That friendship must become our most valued as we prepare here on earth for eternal life.

EASTER SUNDAY MORNING

Here is something else you should know. After Christ died, he rose up out of death. Then our dear Savior lived in this world with his holy apostles, and the risen Christ taught them how to teach all humanity about faith. He showed them how to embrace baptism and reject their former sins. After his resurrection, Jesus ate and drank openly with the disciples. His actions proved to them that he was in fact alive after he had actually died. He substantiated for them that his divine strength had overpowered death.

The risen Christ lived with them forty days. They touched him. With their hands, they held his hands and feet. With their eyes, they saw that Jesus was made of something solid. They inspected the scars on his side, felt his arms and legs, looked at his feet, touched his sides. They knew he had a belly because they watched him eat and drink. They knew he had a tongue because they heard him speak. They held his hands and saw the arms and shoulders on his solid, perfect body.

Nothing was missing, just as he promised. Remember that the kind Savior gave his word to us all that after we die a pilgrim's death, we will also rise up out of death on Doomsday, without losing even the tiniest hair from our earthly bodies.

—Ælfric of Eynsham: *Sermon*

EASTER SUNDAY EVENING

We must get ready then. Our journey requires a rejuvenated faith. We must set high standards. We must rely on the gospel to guide us. It will help us follow Christ and grow better acquainted with him so that we are prepared to live with Jesus in his heavenly kingdom. If we want to live with him there, we must simply do good.

We should ask ourselves the same question David the psalmist asked: "O Lord, who may abide in your tent? Who may dwell on your holy hill?" David hears this answer, and we may share it: "Those who walk blamelessly, and do what is right, and speak the truth from their heart; who do not slander with their tongue, and do no evil to their friends."

We must never think about rejecting God's commandments. We must dedicate ourselves completely to his teaching, and our perseverance will reward us with a knowledge of Christ's own passion. Whoever you are, then, eager to arrive at your Father's heavenly home, follow—with Christ's constant help—the gentle Christian guidelines set down in this little book. They're only a beginning, after all. Amen.

—Benedict: *Rule*

ACKNOWLEDGMENTS

Writing a book is not unlike going to the Scetis desert. It makes you grateful for friends. Once again, Shorter College President Harold E. Newman, Provost L. Craig Shull, and CFO Stephanie Owens have supported my writing through the Scholar-in-Residence position, which lets me hole up with ancient texts. I also thank several colleagues for their invaluable contributions to the Shorter College community. They maintain and constantly upgrade many red-brick, white-columned neoclassical buildings and keep 150 acres well-manicured. Assistant Vice President for Facilities Management Dick Taylor, Director Jeff Agan, Administrative Assistant Diane Sutton, Grounds Supervisor Dennis Pruett, and Bob Bagley, David Bridges, Curtis Brinkley, Jim Long, Ken McClure, and Dennis Waddell make the Hill one of the most beautiful campuses on God's green earth.

I am also grateful to Doris Acevedo for homemade pimento cheese sandwiches, to Gary Davis for being there, to Sabrena Parton for valuable perspicacity, to Bettie Sumner for interlibrary loan assistance, to Phyllis Tickle for wise encouragement, to Rob Wallace for Greek expertise, and to our green-eyed, soft black Manx cat-friend, Lucky, for keeping me company by sleeping under the computer desk at midnight.

I also thank everyone at Paraclete Press for making the book-creating process personal, especially Lil Copan and Jon Sweeney again, for brilliant editing.

I can never thank my family enough. Sean, Kate, and John, I love you.

Appendix A

SHORT BIOGRAPHIES OF FEATURED WRITERS
AND OTHER INFORMATION

Ælfric of Eynsham (ca. 955–ca. 1010). A Benedictine abbot who was the first to translate parts of the Bible into English, Ælfric was also the most influential homilist of his day. His well-written, Christocentric sermons make him a seminal religious English writer.

Angela of Foligno (ca. 1248–1309). Angela lived a hedonistic life before her conversion. When she was forty, her entire family died, and she sold her country villa and gave the profit to the poor. This Franciscan tertiary dictated her conversion story to a distant relative and friar, Brother Arnaldo, in *The Book of the Blessed Angela of Foligno*, the first part of which is called the *Memorial*, describing her passionate love for the "suffering God-man," and the second part of which is called the *Instructions*, containing her teachings.

St. Anselm, Archbishop of Canterbury (ca. 1033–1109). Often called the founder of scholasticism, this Benedictine monk also personally opposed the medieval crusades. He is well-known for his *Prayers* *and Meditations* and *Proslogion,* in which he describes a visual, contemplative praying that nurtures a personal relationship with Christ.

St. Anthony the Great (ca. 251–356). Born into a wealthy family in central Egypt, Anthony sold all he had to follow Christ. His ascetic wisdom was written down in *The Life of St. Anthony* by St. Athanasius of Alexandria. The book was translated into Latin and widely disseminated. This prominent leader of the Desert Fathers is remembered as one of the first desert ascetics and is often called the father of eremitical monasticism.

St. Thomas Aquinas (ca. 1225–1274). This father of the church was an Italian Catholic priest, philosopher, theologian, and writer.

Johann Arndt (1555–1621). This German Lutheran theologian is well-known for having articulated the nature of the mystical union between Christ and his followers.

Abba Arsenius (ca. 354–449). Born into the highest level of Roman society, Arsenius left a life of privilege and sailed for the deserts of Egypt, to learn from Abba John the Dwarf. "Abba" means "Father."

St. Athanasius of Alexandria (ca. 296–373). Called the "Father of Orthodoxy," this Bishop of Alexandria wrote the biography of St. Anthony the Great, *The Life of St. Anthony*, which inspired both Eastern and Western Christian monasticism.

St. Augustine of Hippo (354–430). The son of St. Monica, this church father, also known as the "Doctor of Grace," wrote the first Western spiritual autobiography, the *Confessions*.

St. Basil the Great / Basil of Caesarea (ca. 330–379). The brother of Macrina the Younger and Gregory of Nyssa, Basil was the bishop of Caesarea during difficult times of infighting. He is often considered the founder of Eastern monasticism.

Beatrijs of Nazareth (1200–1268). Taught to read by her mom, she had memorized the Psalms when she was five. At seven, she left her wealthy, religious, well-educated Belgian family to live with the Beguines, later joining the Cistercian nuns at Valle Florida, near Brabant, where she became Prioress in 1236.

St. Benedict of Nursia (ca. 480–ca. 547). Benedict was a sixth-century Italian saint, the founder of the Benedictine order, and the author of the most enduring monastic rule.

St. Bernard of Clairvaux (1090–1153). This French abbot had a major influence on Europe, on the atholic Church, and on the Cistercian monastic order in the first half of the twelfth century.

St. Birgitta of Sweden (1303–1373). Birgitta founded the Order of the Most Holy Savior, or "Brigittines." She was happily married to the Prince of Nericia and was also the mother of eight children. As a cousin to King Magnus, she herself was a member of the Swedish nobility. Her father and husband were both lawyers, and her writing features much legal imagery. She began her career in writing and in politics in her early forties, when she became a widow.

Jacob Boehme or **Jakob Böhme** (1575–1624). Boehme was born in eastern Germany, grew up in the Lutheran Church, and worked as a shoemaker in Görlitz. After a series of mystical visions, he began to write, primarily about the themes of repentance and redemption.

St. Bonaventure (1221–1274). This thirteenth-century friar was a leader in the Franciscan Order. He advised popes, taught at the University of Paris, and in his writings proved himself an inter-disciplinary thinker in theology, psychology, mysticism, and philosophy.

St. John Cassian (ca. 360–435). This Desert Father (and friend of Germanus) was once a monk in a Bethlehem monastery. Then he moved to Egypt to study monasticism.

St. Catherine of Siena (1347–1380). The twenty-fourth of twenty-five children born to a wool-dyer, Catherine took the habit of the *Mantellate*, a group of Dominican lay women, when she was sixteen. By the next year, small pox had disfigured her. But four years later, she experienced a "mystical espousal" with Christ and began caring for the sick and poor, even though she herself knew chronic pain.

St. Clare of Assisi (1194–1253). When she was eighteen, this eldest daughter of a wealthy count heard St. Francis preach and devoted herself to God, but her family opposed her. So she fled in 1212 to become a nun, giving herself to a life of poverty.

Cloud of Unknowing (late fourteenth century). An anonymous English monk wrote this classic work on Christian contemplative prayer. Writing during he same period that Chaucer, Hilton, and Julian of Norwich wrote, the *Cloud*'s author also wrote *Discretion of Stirrings, An Epistle on Prayer,* and *The Book of Privy Counsel.*

Dante Alighieri (1265–1321). This timeless poet's masterpiece, *The Divine Comedy*, describes his journey through Hell, Purgatory, and Paradise, guided by Virgil, by Beatrice, and finally by St. Bernard of Clairvaux. In Dante's native Italy, he is hailed as *il Sommo Poeta* ("the Supreme Poet"). His work is quoted in this devotional because his poetry shows a deep interest in contemplative prayer and its mystical practitioners.

Desert Fathers and Desert Mothers (third century on). These Abbas (Fathers) and Ammas (Mothers) moved into the Scetis desert in Egypt to live as monks and hermits in order to practice an intensely mindful approach to Christlike living. Their wisdom is much prized today as distilling the essence of Christianity into unforgettable stories.

John Donne (1572–1631). Donne was a metaphysical poet, Anglican priest, and Dean of St. Paul's Cathedral in London. Donne wrote religious poetry in the contemplative tradition and therefore belongs in this Lenten devotional.

The Dream of the Rood (eighth century). This Christian crucifixion poem is the earliest dream-vision poem in English. Its author is unknown. Preserved in Old English in the tenth-century

Vercelli Book, parts of this poem are also found on the Ruthwell Cross in Scotland.

St. Elisabeth of Schönau (1129–1165). Born thirty-one years after Hildegard of Bingen and dying at the age of thirty-six, fourteen years before her mentor, Elisabeth corresponded with and visited Hildegard, and they knew each other's work. At twelve, Elisabeth joined a Benedictine monastery; her visions started when she was twenty-three, precipitated by her inner struggle with extreme pain and suicidal depression. She lived in a double monastery, and her community of monks and nuns supported her prayerfully through these episodes.

St. Francis of Assisi (1181–1226). Born in Umbria into a wealthy Italian family, he later embraced the poverty of Christ and became the founder of the Franciscans.

St. Gertrude the Great (1256–ca. 1301). This mystic was born in Saxony. Nothing is known about her family because she was an orphan, appearing at the Cistercian convent of Helfta when she was four years old.

St. Gregory the Great (ca. 540–604). Born into a prominent Roman family, Gregory turned his home into a monastery and became a monk when his father died. Gregory was a reluctant but notable pope from 590 until his death. He sent St. Augustine of Canterbury to England in 596; the only life of St. Benedict of Nursia (in *Dialogues*) is attributed to him; and he composed a classic work, *Pastoral Care* (*Regula Pastoralis*), in which he outlines the responsibilities and concerns of those who minister to others.

St. Gregory of Nyssa (ca. 335–ca. 395). Gregory was the younger brother of Basil and Macrina. Basil appointed him Bishop of Nyssa in 372.

St. Hildegard of Bingen (1098–1179). This remarkable German Benedictine nun was an artist, author, counselor, theologian, dramatist, linguist, naturalist, philosopher, physician, poet, composer, political consultant, prophet, visionary, and founder of monasteries.

Walter Hilton (?–1396). Hilton was an English Augustinian canon, mystic, and author.

St. Ignatius of Loyola (1491–1556). Born in the Basque province of Spain, Ignatius was the founder of the Jesuits. He wrote the *Spiritual Exercises*, a handbook of meditations, prayers, and contem-plative exercises designed to be practiced over the course of a month or incorporated into daily life.

Abba Isaac (fourth century). Born to a poor Egyptian family, this Desert Father became an anchorite in Nitria, south of Scetis, was mentored by Abba Cronius, and later succeeded him as the Priest of El-Qalali (Cells) in 395.

Abba Isidore the Priest (ca. 300–?). This Desert Father was a monk in Scetis, north of Nitria, in Egypt. Scetis is now known as Wadi El Natrun, located in the Western Desert about fifty-six miles northwest of Cairo. Abba Isidore was a friend of Abba Macarius.

St. John Chrysostom (ca. 347–407). This archbishop of Constantinople was well-known as a preacher for social justice, which is why he was posthumously named "Chrysostom," or "Golden-mouthed."

St. John of the Cross (1542–1591). Spanish mystic, Carmelite friar, and friend of St. Teresa of Avila, he was a student of the systematic theology of St. Thomas Aquinas.

Julian of Norwich (1342–1420). An anchoress in Norwich, England, this nun lived through two plagues and England's One Hundred Years' War with France (1337–1453). From her writings, two of her notable teachings are that God is our Mother and that "all will be well."

Thomas à Kempis (ca. 1380–1471). Born near Cologne, Germany (at Kempen), this Renaissance Roman Catholic monk is known for his devotional literature.

Abba Macarius (ca. 300–ca. 390). Once a camel driver, this Egyptian monk visited St. Anthony the Great and was mentored by him. Abba Macarius became one of the original Desert Fathers in Scetis and was later made a priest. His name means "blessed."

St. Macrina the Younger (324–380). Born in Cappadocia, this nun profoundly influenced the Eastern Church, especially her younger brothers, known as the Cappadocian Fathers—Basil the Great and St. Gregory of Nyssa. Macrina lived by the river Iris at Annisa (Turkey's Uluköy) in the Roman province of Pontus. Her grandmother was Macrina the Elder.

Marguerite d'Oingt (ca. 1260–1310). Born into an affluent Lyonnais family, Marguerite became the fourth prioress of the Carthusian convent of Pelotens (now Poleteins) near Lyons.

Mechthild of Magdeburg (ca. 1208–ca. 1282). Born into a noble family of Saxony, Mechthild lived as a Beguine and is known for her writings on the mysticism of divine love.

Abba Moses the Ethiopian (?–ca. 375). Also known as "the Robber," this Desert Father was a former slave and murderer who became a monk and was taught by Isidore the Priest.

Origen (ca. 185–ca. 254). A father of the church, this Alexandrian was a theologian, exegete, and spiritual writer.

Abba Pachomius (ca. 292–346). This skilled monastic leader founded an early *coenobium*, or conventual monastic community, around 320 in Tabennisi in Upper Egypt.

Bishop Palladius (368–ca. 430). The author of the *Lausiac History* (ca. 420), Palladius was a monk from Galatia who later went to Egypt to study the lives of the Desert Fathers.

Abba Poemen (?–ca. 449). His name means "shepherd." In the early fifth century, he probably left Scetis in the Egyptian desert to live in Terenuthis (the present-day Tarrâneh in Egypt).

Pseudo-Dionysius the Areopagite (late fifth or early sixth century). An anonymous Syrian monk—also theologian, mystic, and philosopher in the Christian Neoplatonist tradition—who took the pseudonym of St. Paul's Athenian convert, "Dionysius the Areopagite" (Acts 17:34), to lend his writings more authority.

Richard of St. Victor (?–1173). Prior of the Augustinian abbey of St. Victor in Paris from 1162 until his death in 1173, Richard was originally from Scotland. This twelfth-century theologian was a student of the German mystic Hugo of St. Victor.

Richard Rolle (ca. 1300–1349). Also known as the Hermit of Hampole, the Oxford-educated Rolle was a religious writer, Bible translator, and hermit in rural Yorkshire.

Abba Silvanus (ca. 360–ca. 410). Silvanus was from Palestine and led a small Scetis community in the Western Desert of Egypt.

Amma Syncletica (ca. 380–ca. 460). When Amma Syncletica's parents died, she and her blind sister left their home in Alexandria, Egypt, for the desert. There she eventually became the spiritual director of a Christian community, and many came to her for advice. "Amma" means "Mother."

St. Teresa of Avila (1515–1582). Entering the Carmelite Convent of the Incarnation at Avila in 1535, St. Teresa knew poor health the last forty-five years of her life, from age twenty-one to her death at sixty-six. In 1562, she founded the Convent of Discalced Carmelite Nuns of the Primite Rule of St. Joseph of Avila.

Tertullian (ca. 160–230). Born in Carthage, Tertullian lived there his whole life. He converted to Christianity around the turn of the century and began writing works defending his faith in Christ.

Amma Theodora (fourth century). This Desert Mother lived in the Egyptian deserts. Details about her life are unknown.

Thomas Traherne (ca. 1636–1674). Born in Hereford, England, Traherne was an Oxford-educated parish priest, poet, and religious writer.

Umiltà of Faenza (1226–1310). Born "Rosanese" into a wealthy family, Umiltà knew hardship early on when her father died and her family's finances failed, forcing her to marry against her will at fifteen. When her children died and her husband contracted what was probably a sexually transmitted disease, Umiltà became a Benedictine nun and served as Abbess of Vallombrosen near Florence, Italy. After recovering from his illness, her husband became a monk.

Abba Zosimas (ca. 460–ca. 550). This Palestinian Desert Father is known today for his *Reflections*.

Appendix B

WORKS CONSULTED

Ælfric. MS Cotton Vitellius s.v. Western Manuscripts Room, British Library, London.

Butcher, Carmen Acevedo. *God of Mercy: Ælfric's Sermons and Theology*. Macon, GA: Mercer University Press, 2006.

Chambers, R.W. *On the Continuity of English Prose from Alfred to More and His School*. EETS (Original Series 186a). 1932. London: Oxford University Press, 1950. xlv–clxxiv.

Corpus Christianorum. Turnhout, Belgium: Typographi Brepols, 1953–. *Series Latina* and *Continuatio Mediaevalis* contain twentieth- and twenty-first-century editions of works found in *Patrologia Latina*. Also available online, http://www.corpuschristianorum. org/series/index.html (accessed May 20, 2008).

Gallacher, Patrick J., ed. *The Cloud of Unknowing*. TEAMS, Western Michigan University. Kalamazoo, MI: Medieval Institute Publications, 1997.

Halsall, Paul, ed. *Internet Medieval Sourcebook*. Online Reference Book for Medieval Studies. New York: Fordham University Center for Medieval

Studies. http://www.fordham.edu/halsall/sbook.html (accessed January 13, 2009).

Migne, Jacques-Paul, ed. *Patrologia Cursus Completus. Series Latina, Patrologia Latina (Latin Patrology)*. Paris: Imprimerie Catholique, 1844–55; 1862–65. Volumes 21, 22–30, 32–47, 49–50, 63–64, 66, 73–79, 182–85, 196–97.

Plantinga, Harry, dir. *Christian Classics Ethereal Library*. Grand Rapids, MI: Calvin College. http://www. ccel.org/ (accessed December 14, 2008).

Pope, John C., ed. *Homilies of Ælfric: A Supplementary Collection; Being Twenty-One Full Homilies of His Middle and Later Career For the Most Part Not Previously Edited, with Some Shorter Pieces, Mainly Passages Added to the Second and Third Series*. 2 vols. EETS 259, 260. London: Oxford University Press, 1967, 1968.

Rosweyde, Heribert, ed. *Vitae Patrum*. Books V and VI. 2nd rev. ed. Antwerp: Plantin, 1628. First published by Plantin in 1615.

Schaff, Philip, ed. *The Nicene and Post-Nicene Fathers*. 28 vols. New York: 1889–90.

Schaff, Philip, and Henry Wase, eds. *A Select Library of the Nicene and Post-Nicene Fathers of the Christian Church*. 14 vols. Second Series. Grand Rapids: William B. Eerdmans Publishing Company, 1986–89.

Appendix C

FURTHER READING

Allen, Hope Emily. *English Writings of Richard Rolle*. Oxford: Oxford University Press, 1931.

Allen, Rosamund S. *Richard Rolle: The English Writings*. New York: Paulist Press, 1988.

Anonymous. *The Cloud of Unknowing*. Edited and translated by James Walsh. New York: Paulist Press, 1981.

Arndt, Johann. *True Christianity*. Translated by Peter Erb. New York: Paulist Press, 1979.

Athanasius. *The Life of Antony and the Letter to Marcellinus*. Translated by Robert C. Gregg. New York: Paulist Press, 1980.

Boehme, Jacob. *The Way to Christ*. Translated by Peter Erb. New York: Paulist Press, 1978.

Bonaventure. *The Soul's Journey into God, the Tree of Life, the Life of St. Francis*. Translated by Ewert Cousins. New York: Paulist Press, 1978.

Bourgeault, Cynthia. *Centering Prayer and Inner Awakening*. Lanham, MD: Cowley Publications, 2004.

Budge, Ernest A. Wallis, trans. *The Wit and Wisdom of the Christian Fathers of Egypt*. London: Oxford University Press, 1934.

Butcher, Carmen Acevedo, trans. *The Cloud of Unknowing with the Book of Privy Counsel*. Boston & London: Shambhala, 2009.

———. *Hildegard of Bingen: A Spiritual Reader*. Brewster, MA: Paraclete Press, 2007.

———. *A Little Daily Wisdom*. Brewster, MA: Paraclete Press, 2008.

———. *Man of Blessing: A Life of St. Benedict*. Brewster, MA: Paraclete Press, 2006.

Catherine of Siena. *The Dialogue*. Translated by Suzanne Noffke, OP. New York: Paulist Press, 1980.

———. *The Letters of St. Catherine of Siena*. Translated by Suzanne Noffke, OP. Vol. 1. Binghamton, NY: Medieval & Renaissance Texts & Studies, 1988.

Chadwick, Owen. *Western Asceticism*. Louisville, KY: Westminster John Knox Press, 1979.

Champlin, Joseph M. *The Stations of the Cross with Pope John Paul II*. Liguori, MO: Liguori Publications, 1994.

Christo, George Gus. *St. John Chrysostom on Repentance and Almsgiving*. Washington, DC: Catholic University of America Press, 1997.

Chryssavgis, John. *In the Heart of the Desert: The Spirituality of the Desert Fathers and Mothers*. Bloomington, IN: World Wisdom, 2003.

Clark, John P.H., and Rosemary Dorward. *Walter Hilton: The Scale of Perfection*. New York: Paulist Press, 1990.

Earle, Mary C. *The Desert Mothers: Spiritual Practices from the Women of the Wilderness*. New York: Morehouse, 2007.

Ebor, Donald, ed. *The New English Bible with the Apocrypha*. New York: Cambridge University Press, 1971.

Evans, G.R. *Bernard of Clairvaux: Selected Works*. New York: Paulist Press, 1987.

———. *The Thought of Gregory the Great*. Cambridge: Cambridge University Press, 1986.

Feiss, Hugh. *Essential Monastic Wisdom: Writings on the Monastic Life*. New York: HarperCollins, 1999.

Flanagan, Sabina. *Hildegard of Bingen: A Visionary Life*. New York: Routledge, 2003.

———. *Secrets of God: Writings of Hildegard of Bingen*. Boston & London: Shambhala, 1996.

Flinders, Carol Lee. *Enduring Grace: Living Portraits of Seven Women Mystics*. New York: HarperCollins, 1993.

Forman, Mary. *Praying with the Desert Mothers*. Collegeville, MN: Liturgical Press, 2005.

Foster, Kenelm, OP, and Mary John Ronayne, OP, eds. *I, Catherine: Selected Writings of St. Catherine of Siena*. London: Collins, 1980.

Fox, Matthew, ed. *Hildegard of Bingen's Book of Divine Works with Letters and Songs*. Santa Fe, NM: Bear & Co., 1987.

————. *Illuminations of Hildegard of Bingen*. Rochester, VT: Bear & Co., 2002.

Fry, Timothy. *Rule of Saint Benedict in English*. Collegeville, MN: Liturgical Press, 1982.

Furlong, Monica. *Visions and Longings: Medieval Women Mystics*. Boston & London: Shambhala, 1996.

Greer, Rowan A., trans. *Origen: An Exhortation to Martyrdom, Prayer, and Selected Works*. New York: Paulist Press, 1979.

St. Gregory the Great. *Pastoral Care*. Translated by Henry Davis. New York: Newman Press, 1950.

Gregory of Nyssa. *The Life of Moses*. Translated by Abraham J. Malherbe and Everett Ferguson. New York: Paulist Press, 1978.

Hadewijch. *The Complete Works*. Translated by Mother Columba Hart, OSB. New York: Paulist Press, 1980.

Hannay, James O. *The Wisdom of the Desert*. London: Methuen & Co., 1904. University of Notre Dame, Jacques Maritain Center. http://maritain.nd.edu/jmc/etext/wd.htm (accessed May 27, 2008).

Hildegard of Bingen. *The Book of the Rewards of Life (Liber Vitae Meritorum)*. Translated by Bruce W. Hozeski. New York: Garland, 1994.

————. *Scivias*. Translated by Mother Columba Hart, OSB, and Jane Bishop. New York: Paulist Press, 1990.

John of the Cross. *Selected Writings*. Translated by Kiernan Kavanaugh. New York: Paulist Press, 1987.

Julian of Norwich. *Showings*. Translated by Edmund Colledge, OSA, and James Walsh, SJ. New York: Paulist Press, 1978.

Kezel, Albert Ryle, trans. *Birgitta of Sweden: Life and Selected Revelations*. New York: Paulist Press, 1990.

McAvoy, Jane. *Communion with the Friends of God: Meditations and Prayers from Women Mystics*. St. Louis, MO: Chalice Press, 2001.

McKenna, Megan. *The New Stations of the Cross: The Way of the Cross According to Scripture*. New York: Image Book, 2003.

Mechthild of Magdeburg. *The Flowing Light of the Godhead*. Translated by Frank Tobin. New York: Paulist Press, 1998.

Merton, Thomas, trans. *The Wisdom of the Desert: Sayings from the Desert Fathers of the Fourth Century*. Boston & London: Shambhala, 2004.

Muccilli, Rev. Sebastian L. *Stations of the Cross*. Erie, PA: Pax Christi U.S.A., 2006. http://www.paxchris tiusa.org/StationsoftheCross.pdf (accessed March 26, 2008).

Obbard, Elizabeth Ruth, ed. *Medieval Women Mystics: Selected Spiritual Writings*. New York: New City Press, 2002.

Peers, E. Allison. *Dark Night of the Soul: A Masterpiece in the Literature of Mysticism by St. John of the Cross*. New York: Image Book, 1959.

Petersen, Joan M. *Handmaids of the Lord: Contemporary Descriptions of Feminine Asceticism in the First Six Christian Centuries*. Kalamazoo, MI: Cistercian Publications, 1996.

Pseudo-Athanasius. *The Life and Regimen of the Blessed and Holy Teacher, Syncletica*. Translated by Elizabeth Bongie. Toronto: Peregrina Publishing Co., 1995.

Riedel, Ingrid. *Hildegard von Bingen: Prophetin der kosmis chen Weisheit*. Stuttgart: Kreuz Verlag, 1994.

Ruether, Rosemary Radford. *Visionary Women: Three Medieval Mystics*. Minneapolis, MN: Augsburg Fortress, 2002.

Swan, Laura. *The Forgotten Desert Mothers: Sayings, Lives, and Stories of Early Christian Women*. New York: Paulist Press, 2001.

Sweeney, Jon. *Cloister Talks: Learning from My Friends the Monks*. Wheaton, IL: Brazos, 2009.

————. *The St. Francis Prayer Book: A Guide to Deepen Your Spiritual Life*. Orleans, MA: Paraclete Press, 2004.

Ward, Benedicta, trans. *The Desert Fathers: Sayings of the Early Christian Monks*. New York: Penguin Books, 2003.

————. *The Prayers and Meditations of Saint Anselm with the Proslogion*. 1973. London: Penguin Books, 1986.

————. *The Sayings of the Desert Fathers*. Kalamazoo, MI: Cistercian Publications, 1975, 1984.

Warnke, Frank J. *John Donne*. New York: Twayne Publishers, 1987.

Zinn, Grover A., trans. *Richard of St. Victor: The Book of the Patriarchs, the Mystical Ark, Book Three of the Trinity*. New York: Paulist Press, 1979.

INTRODUCTION

x *"Each fasted forty days. . . .'blessed are all those who wait for him.'"* Isaiah 30:18.

xi *"To introduce you further to each voice . . . is provided in Appendix A."* In addition to the short biographies found in Appendix A, Appendix B lists Works Consulted, and Appendix C provides a Further Reading section.

xii *"Their tried-and-true principles can guide us . . . 'shall walk and not faint.'"* Isaiah 40:31.

xiv *"As we read 1 Corinthians, . . . grow up."* 1 Corinthians 13:11.

xv *"Veronica wipes the face of Jesus."* Legends speak of Veronica or Sheraphia, the wife of a powerful Sanhedrin member.

xvi *"Megan McKenna outlines these modern scriptural stations in her book. . . .'"* Megan McKenna, *The New Stations of the Cross: The Way of the Cross According to Scripture* (New York: Image Book, 2003), viii, 116–21.

xviii *"The monk Thomas Merton . . . 'open to unforeseen conclusions.'"* McKenna, *New Stations of the Cross,* x.

xix *"As Matthew writes in his Gospel: . . . 'Or what will they give in return for their life?'"* Matthew 16:25–26.

xx *"Instead, let Christ strengthen you with his heavenly courage."* See the Maundy Thursday Evening devotional for more of Thomas à Kempis.

xxi *"David sang about this in the Psalms: 'Happy are those . . . go from strength to strength.'"* Psalm 84:5, 7a.

xxi *"He is the only one who can make us happy."* See the Second Sunday Evening of Lent devotional for more of John of the Cross.

xxi *"As Karol Wojtyla wrote . . . 'which the world does not reveal to me.'"* McKenna, *New Stations of the Cross*, x.

xxiv *"These latter two verses strengthen Station One's theme, reminding us that we are lethargic, mortal. . . ."* In the introductory paragraphs for each station, where Christ's last moments are described and their meaning contemplated, the alert reader will notice that I have made a conscious effort to shift the verbs used in these paragraphs from the expected past tense (which would refer to Jesus as a historical person) to the present tense, intimating the real, abiding presence of Christ in our lives and nurturing in us all ongoing reflection on this mystery that transcends time.

xxxi *"When we falter, the Spirit helps us, . . . 'with sighs too deep for words.'"* Romans 8:26.

xxxi *"The Christian authors quoted in this book . . . the quiet the psalmist recommends."* Psalm 32:3.

xxxi *"With this book, we can make . . . with him: 'Be still, and know that I am God!'"* Psalm 32:6–7; 46:10.

xxxii *"By spending time with them, . . . 'take up their cross and follow me.'"* Matthew 16:24.

xxxv *"As Father Laurence Freeman pointed out in a sermon for All Souls Day . . . 'of Christ.'"* Cynthia Bourgeault, *Centering Prayer and Inner Awakening* (Lanham, MD: Cowley Publications, 2004), 81.

xxxvi "If then there is any encouragement . . . even death on a cross."
Philippians 2:1–8.

xxxvii "Simply reach out to the never-aloof God, and discover . . . 'you
are yourself.'" Bourgeault, *Centering Prayer*, 6.

xxxix "As a last reminder of the transformative . . . 'you redeemed the
world.'" McKenna, *New Stations of the Cross*, xviii.

FIRST STATION

5 "We need a certain brokenness of heart, . . . 'good news brought
to them.'" Luke 7:22b.

7 "It is as if they are saying as they cling to the moment, 'It is good
for us to be here.'" This sentence points out the transformative qualities of spending time with God; "It is
good for us to be here" are Peter's words as he, James,
and John witness Jesus' transfiguration: "Lord, it is
good for us to be here." See Matthew 17:3–4.

9 "The book of Romans tells us to wake up: . . . 'wake from sleep.'"
Romans 13:11.

9 "For the Gospel of John says, 'Walk . . . may not overtake you.'"
John 12:35.

SECOND STATION

13 "Jesus said, . . . 'there are some who do not believe.'"
John 6:64.

13 "'Because of . . . went about with him.'" John 6:66.

13 "Then Jesus asked . . . 'wish to go away.'" John 6:67.

14 "Peter answered . . . 'the Holy One of God.'"
John 6:68–69.

17 "If this were not so, the best teacher . . . 'and humble in heart.'"
Matthew 11:29.

21 *"Jesus said, 'See, I am sending you out like sheep . . . innocent as doves.'"* Matthew 10:16.

THIRD STATION

29 *"Speak to your Creator, saying, 'Your face, LORD, do I seek.'"* Psalm 27:8.

FOURTH STATION

34 *"This is the man who said to Christ, . . . 'I will not deny you.'"* Mark 14:31.

37 *"Follow the Lord instead; . . . 'the will of him who sent me.'"* John 6:38.

38 *"The Lord himself set us an example . . . 'He became obedient to the point of death.'"* Philippians 2:8.

38 *"As the Psalm says, 'Wait for the LORD, be strong, . . . wait for the LORD!'"* Psalm 27:14.

38 *"They keep St. Paul's words in mind . . . 'conquerors through him who loved us.'"* Romans 8:37.

38 *"Proverbs says, 'When words are many, transgression is not lacking.'"* Proverbs 10:19.

42 *"Remember that in the Sermon on the Mount Jesus said, 'Blessed are the merciful.'"* Matthew 5:7.

42 *"Looking down on us as we climb the ladder of humility, Jesus, . . . 'I will give you rest.'"* Matthew 11:28.

43 *"The Gospel calls poverty . . . buy that field."* See Matthew 13:44.

44 *"As we read in Philippians, . . . 'every knee should bend.'"* Philippians 2:8–10.

44 *"Humility is a lowly nothingness . . . 'through all and in all.'"* Ephesians 4:4–6.

45 *David sang about this . . .* "'They go from strength to strength.'" Psalm 84:5, 7a.

46 *"In dialogue with God, we learn that . . . 'those who humble themselves will be exalted.'"* Luke 14:11.

FIFTH STATION

49 *"How great a forest . . . tongue—a restless evil, full of deadly poison."* James 3:5b–8.

49 *Shakespeare's Hamlet . . .* "'Words, words, words.'" Hamlet II, ii, 192.

51 *"We read in Judges, . . . 'It is too wonderful.'"* Judges 13:17–18.

51 *"On the other hand, Christians give this Name many names . . . nothing that has been created."* See Exodus 3:14; John 14:6; John 8:12; Genesis 28:13; John 14:6; Matthew 19:17; Psalm 27:4; Romans 16:27; Isaiah 5:1; Psalm 136:2–3; Isaiah 6:3; John 3:16; Exodus 3:14; Genesis 1; Genesis 1:20; John 1:10; Proverbs 8:1; 1 Corinthians 2:16; John 1:1; Psalm 44:21; Colossians 2:3; Revelation 19:1; Revelation 1:5; Revelation 17:14; Daniel 7:9; Psalm 102:27; Exodus 15:2; Jeremiah 23:6; 1 Corinthians 1:30; Isaiah 40:15; 1 Kings 19:12; see Psalm 84:11; Revelation 22:16; Deuteronomy 4:24; Psalm 84:6; John 4:24; Acts 2:2; Hosea 14:5; Exodus 13:21; Psalm 118:22; Psalm 31:2–3; and 1 Corinthians 15:28.

SIXTH STATION

63 *"This is so like what happens when we try to light . . . God within."* Hebrew 12:29.

67 *"Remember Abraham's words to the rich man in hell: . . . 'has been fixed.'"* Luke 16:26.

67 *"As the prophet Jeremiah said, 'Death has come up into our windows.'"* Jeremiah 9:21.

69 *"And if we could sustain this not-thinking . . . 'the joy of your master.'"* Matthew 25:23

SEVENTH STATION

76 *"It answers the question St. Paul asked . . . 'in whom have they not believed?'"* Joel 2:32; Romans 10:14.

79 *"When you love the Lord your God with all your heart, soul, mind, and strength. . . ."* See Deuteronomy 6:4–5; Mark 12:30.

80 *"'Love your neighbor as yourself' includes loving your enemies."* Matthew 19:19

80 *"Remember that Jesus said: 'Do good to those who hate you.'"* Luke 6:27.

80 *"We must endure in love, always remembering . . . 'His intention toward me was love.'"* Song of Solomon 2:4.

EIGHTH STATION

83 *"I was hungry and you gave me food, . . . you did it to me."* Matthew 25:35–36, 40.

85 *"Remember that the Bible says, 'We are all one body.'"* 1 Corinthians 12:13.

90 *"Christ chose to have parents who were financially poor . . .' stronger than the human strength.'"* 1 Corinthians 1:25.

91 *"Peter said so: 'For to this you have been called, . . . follow in his steps.'"* 1 Peter 2:21.

92 *"As St. Paul said, 'For the message about the cross . . . is the power of God.'"* 1 Corinthians 1:18.

92 *"God is our partner, for, as St. Paul says in his letter to the Romans. . . ."* See Romans 8:28.

92 *"To continue on this path with Christ . . . 'I die every day!'"*
1 Corinthians 15:31.

93 *"These words are intended for anyone . . . 'but forfeit their life?'"*
Matthew 16:26.

NINTH STATION

97 *"They emphasize the tragic suffering . . . 'for your children.'"*
Luke 23:28

98 *"Have mercy on me, O God, . . . and sustain in me a willing
spirit."* Psalm 51:1–12.

102 *"This house is Christ, as we read: Our 'life is hidden with Christ
in God.'"* Colossians 3:3.

105 *"As David prayed in the Psalms, . . . 'Have mercy on me, O
God.'"* Psalm 51:1.

106 *"St. Paul engaged in contemplative prayer . . . 'and him crucified.'"*
1 Corinthians 2:2.

106 *"He also said, 'May I never boast of anything . . . and I to the
world.'"* Galatians 6:14.

TENTH STATION

109 *"He was despised and rejected . . . . and by his bruises we are
healed."* Isaiah 53:3–5.

110 *"In the book Song of Solomon, we read, 'Let me see your face.'"*
Song of Solomon 2:14.

111 *"You revived him because your love, kind Lord, is as strong as
death."* See Song of Solomon 8:6.

111 *"The Son of Man said, 'When I am lifted up from the earth, . . .
to myself.'"* John 12:32.

116 *"Remember, Jesus commanded: 'Do not judge, so that you may
not be judged.'"* Matthew 7:1.

117 *"The first letter of John says, 'All who hate a brother or sister are murderers.'"* 1 John 3:15.

119 *"Be as compassionate and as purposeful as a doctor setting a broken bone."* See Galatians 6:1: *"Restore* [each other] in a spirit of gentleness." *Restore* is from the Greek *katartizo,* "to set a broken bone," also "to mend nets or outfit a boat." As Shorter College religion professor Rob Wallace pointed out in a conversation, *katartizo* can also signify "'to complete' the education of a child, acknowledging that he or she is now free to lead an adult life." In other words, discipleship is mending one's ways and preparing to go out into the world, in love. See Mark 1:19.

ELEVENTH STATION

122 *"In his conversaion . . . 'For my yoke is easy, and my burden is light.'"* Matthew 11:28–30.

123 *"We are also the other . . . 'Save yourself and us!'"* Luke 23:39

125 *"What does it mean to be 'made in God's image'?"* Genesis 1:27.

125 *"We read in Ephesians: 'Be renewed in the spirit of your minds . . . in true righteouness and holiness.'"* Ephesians 4:23–24.

125 *"At creation, the triune God emphasized . . . 'according to our likeness.'"* Genesis 1:26a.

131 *"Jesus said, 'Do not store . . . where thieves break in and steal.'"* Matthew 6:19.

TWELFTH STATION

135 *"As we read in 1 Timothy, . . . 'with absolute purity.'"*
1 Timothy 5:1–2.

143 *Palm, or Passion, Sunday Morning.* Palm, or Passion, Sunday honors Christ's entry into Jerusalem on a donkey, as we read in Matthew 21:5–10:

> "Tell the daughter of Zion, Look, your king is coming to you, humble, and mounted on a donkey, and on a colt, the foal of a donkey." The disciples went and did as Jesus had directed them; they brought the donkey and the colt, and put their cloaks on them, and he sat on them. A very large crowd spread their cloaks on the road, and others cut branches from the trees and spread them on the road. The crowds that went ahead of him and that followed were shouting, "Hosanna to the Son of David! Blessed is the one who comes in the name of the Lord! Hosanna in the highest heaven!" When he entered Jerusalem, the whole city was in turmoil, asking, "Who is this?"

It may seem, at first consideration, that Palm Sunday is out of place here under the twelfth station, meditating on Jesus on the cross, with his mother and disciple below, but this double exposure of events is a reminder that, like life, Lent's prayerful journey is not a linear path but one that often doubles back on itself in reflection; plus, the stations of the cross and the liturgical year do not align in a strict chronological sense because of the stations' strong emphasis on the redemptive suffering of Jesus and those events in his life. The theme of Station Twelve is "The Community of Agape Love," and although we believe we know that Jesus Christ is the Son of God, we do well to join this community of dusty city dwellers of Jerusalem, asking in awe and surprise as Christ rides past on a humble donkey, "Who is this?"

144 *"He came looking for his lost sheep, ... 'to save the lost.'"* Luke 19:10.

THIRTEENTH STATION

147 *"We remember that Job . . . 'come forth from the womb and expire?'"* Job 3:9–11.

147 *"Where were you when I . . . Anyone who argues with God must respond."* Job 38:4–11; 39:26–27; 40:2.

148 *"Job's response is to God's questioning the beginning of wisdom . . . 'Hear and I will speak.'"* Job 42:3–4.

152 *"Hear my prayer, O LORD, . . . established in your presence."* Psalm 102.

154 *"The Creator is invisible, . . . 'to the end of the world.'"* Psalm 19:1, 4.

158 *"See how Christ gave himself . . . 'for your hearts here.'"* See Matthew 11:29.

159 *Maundy Thursday Morning.* "Maundy Thursday" comes from the Latin for the "new commandment" [*mandatum novum*] that Jesus gave his disciples: "Love one another," as we read in the Gospel of John:

> [Jesus] got up from the table, took off his outer robe, and tied a towel around himself. Then he

poured water into a basin and began to wash the
disciples' feet and to wipe them with the towel that
was tied around him. . . . After he had washed their
feet, had put on his robe, and had returned to the
table, he said to them, "Do you know what I have
done to you? You call me Teacher and Lord—and
you are right, for that is what I am. So if I, your
Lord and Teacher, have washed your feet, you also
ought to wash one another's feet. For I have set
you an example, that you also should do as I have
done to you. Very truly, I tell you, servants are
not greater than their master, nor are messengers
greater than the one who sent them. If you know
these things, you are blessed if you do them. . . . I
give you a new commandment, that you love one
another. Just as I have loved you, you also should
love one another." John 13:4–5, 12–17, 34

As with Palm (or Passion) Sunday earlier, it may be non-
linear to observe Station Thirteen's "Jesus dies on the
cross" here at Maundy Thursday, but the juxtaposition
of the two events emphasizes that as Jesus washes his disciples' feet, he is showing them that the way of the cross
is servanthood and the emptying called *kenosis* that Paul
describes in Philippians 2. The "new commandment" is
that we must wash each other's feet, die for each other,
and empty ourselves of self in the service of Christ, by
trusting in him and listening to his commands.

161 *"Let the same mind . . . even death on a cross."*
Philippians 2:5–8.

161 *"I was looking for Christ-centered knowledge, but I was blind. . . ."* Luke 10:21.

162 *"John Donne:* Holy Sonnet X." A classic text on John Donne's metaphysical poetry is Frank J. Warnke, *John Donne* (New York: Twayne Publishers, 1987).

FIFTEENTH STATION

173 *"We should ask ourselves . . . 'Who may dwell on yor holy hill?'"* Psalm 15:1.

173 *"David hears this answer, . . . 'do no evil to their friends.'"* Psalm 15:2–3.